Reviving Rhetoric Across the Curriculum

A timeless tool for effective communication, civic participation and a means to deciphering the human condition, rhetoric is now enjoying a revival in schools. This book positions rhetoric as an essential component of the curriculum, helping learners to read and think critically, listen actively and speak persuasively. It shows how rhetoric empowers young people with the knowledge and skills to become informed and critical citizens.

Drawing on the authors' expertise in teaching, curriculum design and academic research, the book considers what it means to teach rhetoric and why there is a rationale to do so with fidelity. It also offers guidance for implementing rhetoric across the curriculum. It offers a progression model to help students understand the social structures of language through the subjects they already study with a sensitivity to the subject content.

Essential reading for teachers and school leaders, this pioneering text provides everything needed to revive rhetoric in schools, enabling students to thrive both academically and in the wider world.

Arlene Holmes-Henderson is Professor of Classics Education and Public Policy at Durham University. She is an award-winning qualified schoolteacher, and she taught classical subjects (Latin, Greek and Classical Studies) in secondary schools for more than a decade. Her doctoral thesis examined the role of rhetoric in 21st-century educational policy and practice. By sharing her expertise on ancient rhetoric with policymakers and teachers, she has secured several policy changes in English education which widen access to high-quality rhetoric, oracy and spoken language education. She is the author of 7 books and more than 50 articles. Arlene was awarded an MBE for Services to Education in 2023 and in 2026 was awarded the Classical Association Prize in recognition of her success in widening access to the study of the ancient world.

Kat Howard is Executive School Improvement Lead and Curriculum and Assessment Lead at a Multi Academy Trust, working with schools across the West Midlands region and leading curriculum and assessment across the Trust. She is also founding CEO of LitdriveUK, a charity and subject association dedicated to providing resources and CPD provision for English teachers and tutors. She is the author of the bestseller *Stop Talking About Wellbeing: A Pragmatic Approach to Teacher Workload* and co-author of another bestseller, *Symbiosis: The Curriculum and the Classroom.*

Reviving Rhetoric Across the Curriculum

A Guide for Teachers and School Leaders

Arlene Holmes-Henderson and Kat Howard

Routledge
Taylor & Francis Group
LONDON AND NEW YORK

Designed cover image: © Getty Images

First published 2027
by Routledge
4 Park Square, Milton Park, Abingdon, Oxon OX14 4RN

and by Routledge
605 Third Avenue, New York, NY 10158

Routledge is an imprint of the Taylor & Francis Group, an informa business

For Product Safety Concerns and Information please contact our EU representative GPSR@taylorandfrancis.com. Taylor & Francis Verlag GmbH, Kaufingerstraße 24, 80331 München, Germany.

British Library Cataloguing-in-Publication Data
A catalogue record for this book is available from the British Library

ISBN: 978-1-032-52902-8 (hbk)
ISBN: 978-1-032-52903-5 (pbk)
ISBN: 978-1-003-40906-9 (ebk)

DOI: 10.4324/9781003409069

Typeset in Melior
by KnowledgeWorks Global Ltd.

Contents

About the authors

Arlene Holmes-Henderson is Professor of Classics Education and Public Policy at Durham University. She is an award-winning qualified schoolteacher, and she taught classical subjects (Latin, Greek and Classical Studies) in secondary schools for more than a decade. Her doctoral thesis examined the role of rhetoric in 21st-century educational policy and practice. By sharing her expertise on ancient rhetoric with policymakers and teachers, she has secured several policy changes in English education which widen access to high-quality rhetoric, oracy and spoken language education. She is the author of 7 books and more than 50 articles. Arlene was awarded an MBE for Services to Education in 2023 and in 2026 was awarded the Classical Association Prize in recognition of her success in widening access to the study of the ancient world.

Kat Howard is Executive School Improvement Lead and Curriculum and Assessment Lead at a Multi Academy Trust, working with schools across the West Midlands region and leading curriculum and assessment across the Trust. She is also founding CEO of LitdriveUK, a charity and subject association dedicated to providing resources and CPD provision for English teachers and tutors. She is the author of the bestseller *Stop Talking About Wellbeing: A Pragmatic Approach to Teacher Workload* and co-author of another bestseller, *Symbiosis: The Curriculum and the Classroom.*

Acknowledgements

This book would have been impossible without the generosity of classroom practitioners, who share their experiences in Chapters 4 and 5. Thank you to Matt Pinkett and Cristobal Rodriguez-Casado. Their willingness to contribute is testament to their professionalism and their belief in the power of rhetoric in education.

This book had a long gestation. Kat is a busy trust leader, and Arlene is an academic with runs several concurrent projects. Our families and friends have been understanding when we needed to carve out time in evenings and weekends to bring the book to fruition. We thank them.

Finally, our thoughts on rhetoric have developed and evolved as a result of interaction with colleagues at training events, conferences and social media. In particular, we'd like to thank Martin Robinson and Mary Myatt, Dr Tom F Wright (University of Sussex), Dr Anne-Grete Kaldahl (OsloMet University) and Dr Janja Zmavc (Educational Research Institute, Ljubljana). Equally, thank you to Claire Hill (Steplab), Helena Brothwell (Windsor Academy Trust) and Dr Dan Owen (Ofsted) for influencing and informing the thinking behind Part B.

Glossary and abbreviations

We write with a mindfulness that the education sector is crammed with a number of terms that would be deemed as jargon, or indeed, that have evolved over time and so therefore carry multiple meanings. To support the reader experience, a glossary below aims to provide our definitions as authors, with a health warning that we know universal meanings for many of these terms do not exist. Such is the glorious and contentious work of schools, curriculum and leadership!

Term	Definition
canons of speech	The five classical principles for effective communication: Invention (finding arguments/ideas), Arrangement (structuring the message), Style (word choice/language), Memory (knowing the content), and Delivery (voice, gestures, presence).
citizenship	The knowledge and skills needed to participate actively and responsibly in society
critical literacy	Questioning and analyzing texts to understand the relationship between language, power and social context.
critical thinking	Evaluating evidence to form reasoned judgements and sound decisions.
democratic deliberation	Deliberation offers citizens with opposing views the opportunity to explain and justify the foundations of their beliefs in an effort to transform the alternative opinions held by fellow deliberators. All sides can then reach new and acceptable positions for collective action.
dialectic	Dialectic is a a process to agree a definition of something by referring to opposites in a discursive, step-by-step process of reasoning. It involves the exchange of questions and answers.

Term	Definition
disinformation	Disinformation is false or misleading information that is deliberately created and spread to deceive, manipulate or secure political or economic gain, and which may cause public harm.
ethopoeia	A technique which requires orators to put themselves in the place of others and give a speech as another character.
ethos	How a speaker cultivates credibility and authenticity in order to persuade.
gravitas	One of the ancient Roman virtues. It can mean seriousness, weight, dignity and importance. It also conveys a sense of responsibility and commitment to the task.
implementation	The process of executing a plan, informed by a vision. All stakeholders are assigned specific activities as part of an implementation plan so that roles and responsibilities are as part of a collective effort to enact the plan effectively.
logos	The arguments and evidence used by a speaker in order to persuade.
malinformation	Malinformation is defined as factual information that is shared with the intent to cause harm, often by taking it out of its original context or by publishing private material.
misinformation	Misinformation is incorrect information which is typically spread unintentionally, mostly caused by a lack of knowledge or simply a misunderstanding,
oracy	Effective spoken communication and active listening. From the Latin 'ora' meaning 'mouth'.
orator	A public speaker who is skilled at communicating effectively.
pathos	How a speaker connects emotionally with the audience; building a rapport in order to persuade.
rationale	A clear reason that underpins a curriculum vision and principles, outlining why selections and also omissions feature. A clear rationale for curriculum at school or system level provides teachers and leaders with a shared language to make curriculum-relevant decisions.
refutatio	The act of disproving an argument, claim or theory, where a speaker addresses and counters an opponent's points with evidence or logic.

(Continued)

Term	Definition
rhetor	A teacher of rhetoric in the ancient world; a persuasive speaker.
rhetoric	An ancient framework for persuasive argumentation.
rhetorical framework	A sequence of steps for persuasive communication including (*exordium* – introduction; *narratio* – background information; *divisio* – points to be covered in the argument; *confirmatio* – the argument, supported by evidence; *refutatio* – engagement with, and response to, opponents' arguments; *peroratio* – conclusion).
rhetorical techniques/devices	Linguistic patterns used in writing or speaking to persuade an audience, evoke emotion or make an argument more compelling.
sophists/sophistry	Sophists were influential teachers in ancient Greece (5th-4th centuries BCE) who provided practical education, especially rhetoric, to young men for success in politics and public life. They emphasized skills like debate, critical thinking, and oratory. Plato accused them of prioritizing winning arguments over truth.
theory of change	A way to depict how and why change will happen, making explicit how implementation activities are linked to tangible intended long term outcomes.

Foreword: Martin Robinson

Oracy is the latest buzzword in education. Substacks, blog posts, books, INSET days and government diktats are dedicated to it. Yet there is widespread confusion about what the term actually means, how it translates into classroom practice, and controversy about whether it smuggles in a deficit model, one in which class, race and regionality are judged against an idea of speaking 'properly'. In reaction to this, we are sometimes invited to swing to the opposite extreme: to encourage people simply to 'find their own voice', whether or not that voice is intelligible, accountable or meaningful beyond the self.

This book cuts through that confusion by focusing not on identity, but on words. The authors, the excellent and eloquent Arlene and Kat, make a profoundly persuasive argument that this is the time for education to take rhetoric seriously again: not as performance, not as spin and certainly not as an ornamental extra, but as an essential way to build judgement and eloquence. The book suggests that rhetoric has been displaced by exam-driven functional literacy, generic oracy programmes and a suspicion of rhetoric as an empty art wielded by bad faith actors. The result has been a weakening of students' capacity for critical thinking and their agency.

Reviving Rhetoric Across the Curriculum is not a nostalgic call to return to a classical curriculum, nor is it a fashionable intervention dressed up as innovation. Instead, it asks a more demanding question: what happens to teaching, learning and curriculum design when we accept that reading, writing and speaking are ethical and democratic acts, not merely technical ones?

The authors are clear that rhetoric is not just about teaching children how to persuade others. It is about teaching them how arguments work, how language shapes meaning, how audiences are propositioned and how responsibility sits alongside expression. In a system that oscillates between celebrating 'posh voices' on the one hand and policing language on the other, this feels both timely and necessary.

What makes this book particularly valuable is its refusal to treat rhetoric as a bolt-on. Rhetoric here is not simply an oracy programme, a writing framework or a set of techniques to boost exam performance, though it may serve those ends. The argument is far richer: rhetoric is integral to curriculum coherence – the way knowledge, language and reasoning develop together over time. When rhetoric is taught well, students are not merely fluent; they are discerning. In a world saturated by persuasive voices, through online spaces, political rhetoric and social pressure, students need to be able to distinguish what is valuable from what is manipulative, misleading or downright dangerous. This book gives teachers the tools to make that difference.

The book weaves together classical rhetorical thought, classroom practice, curriculum design and professional reflection. It treats teachers as thoughtful professionals. It does not patronise them, nor does it assume they can only engage with simple content. It assumes that teachers are capable of engaging with rich ideas, not just implementing strategies. Rhetoric's place in the curriculum is treated not as a delivery mechanism, but as an expression of educational purpose.

As I argued in Trivium 21c, the main job of a school is not simply to secure results, but to help provide meaning. This book quotes that idea and, more importantly, takes it seriously by working through its implications with care and intellectual honesty. Rhetoric, as presented here, is not a luxury. It is an entitlement. To be able to compose, listen to, challenge and judge arguments is fundamental to participation in a democratic society. When students are denied access to these tools, inequality operates at the level of language itself leading to disenfranchisement.

This book will reward readers who are willing to think, to question habits and to resist the latest educational fashions. It does not merely hark back to a great tradition; it brings that tradition decisively up to date. For teachers and leaders seeking to reconnect language, knowledge and purpose, *Reviving Rhetoric* takes seriously Zeno's claim that rhetoric is the art that enables us to reach out to the world with an open hand.

I can't recommend it enough.

Martin Robinson

PART A
Theory and research: The compelling argument for rhetoric as integral to curriculum

1 Why rhetoric matters now

From the outset, we want to stress that the focus on rhetoric is not a politicisation of the curriculum and should not be treated or perceived as such: the use of such a framework draws on the origins of a discipline. Our book focuses on Western traditions of rhetoric without making any value judgements about its relationship to other global rhetorics. There is a universality to rhetoric that enables us to present a 'windows and mirrors' approach to belonging within our curriculum offer.

In this first chapter, we outline how rhetoric provides a means for pupils to interrogate the contemporary communication they encounter using a range of perspectives, for example, historical narrative, geographical/sociological bias and critique of both the spoken and the written word. This helps learners to understand the political and social environment within which they operate as citizens. To be able to navigate these spheres with confidence, both academically and vocationally, leaders, teachers and learners will need both parts of this book. Section A focuses on the research base for rhetorical education, and Section B provides models for integrating it across school curricula. We have a responsibility to reveal the 'wizard behind the curtain' to enable pupils to navigate communicative complexity and empower them to operate effectively within this arena.

Why do we need rhetoric in the curriculum?

Changes to the way that we digest and exchange information and changes to the role and form of language mean that children are now exposed to more information than ever before, and they can become somewhat desensitised to it. We believe that teaching rhetoric gives learners the tools to read between the lines, question authorship and identify bias, but it also helps them to articulate their own interpretation of the world.

COVID-19 exacerbated the problem of fake news. *Dr Tedros Adhanom Ghebreyesus*, Director-General of the World Health Organisation, declared in February 2020 that COVID-19 was not the only public health emergency the world was facing – he said

DOI: 10.4324/9781003409069-2

that we were also suffering from an 'infodemic: fake news spreads faster and more easily than this virus, and is just as dangerous'.

The Westminster government issued official SHARE advice (https://www.gov.uk/government/news/government-cracks-down-on-spread-of-false-coronavirus-information-online) to all members of the public to help them establish whether communications they encounter may be misleading:

- Source – make sure information comes from a trusted source
- Headline – always read beyond the headline
- Analyse – check the facts
- Retouched – does the image or video look as though it has been doctored?
- Error – look out for bad grammar and spelling

This is a shortened and diluted version of the rhetorical method. Rhetoric helps young people to consider the use of language to persuade, the credibility of the speaker and how gestures affect emotional response. Rhetoric informs the wider curriculum: providing epistemic ascent where it may be lacking not just in English language qualifications but in all subjects. As we'll show in Chapters 2 and 3, building rhetoric into your school curriculum can safeguard young people against fake news, misinformation, disinformation and malinformation, for example, in the overwhelming 'noise' about vaccines, extremism and politics. It boosts their ability to speak, protest, negotiate, argue and listen actively. At a time when large language models are generating written texts, rhetoric equips citizens to go beyond AI's abilities and communicate using human-specific characteristics, for example, rapport, community building and emotional engagement. We are reminded of this: 'If you talk to a man in a language he understands, that goes to his head. If you talk to him in his language, that goes to his heart' (Nelson Mandela).

Rhetorical pedagogy today

Where rhetoric is currently taught, it is viewed through different lenses. In the Classics classroom, the study of rhetoric involves the close analysis of classical literature in Latin and Greek, investigating how the author has used rhetorical frameworks and techniques to communicate in a particular way. Several times in its long history, the study of rhetoric has contracted to simply the study of style, consisting of memorising long lists of techniques (Bizzell and Herzberg 1990: 6). Conversely, we believe that the study of rhetoric is a far richer and more diverse discipline than simply learning lists of rhetorical techniques, although familiarity with these is an important stage in the learning process. Knowledge of rhetoric helps interrogate the impact of communication and facilitates improved understanding of authors' motivations. In Latin and Greek, students encounter the basic elements of classical rhetorical theory, but this is limited to the deconstruction of prose and verse literature. They are not required to create or deliver an argument.

In the USA, rhetoric is viewed through a different lens. Sometimes called 'writing across the curriculum', rhetoric appears as a first year course in almost half of the universities in North America (Bourelle 2009: 35). Taught, in the main, by English instructors, this brand of rhetorical education is often linked to improving expression in academic writing (Berlin 1988, Fleming 1988, Berlin 1996, Booth 2004) and has developed since the 1970s as a composition course to combat poor literacy levels among high school graduates upon arrival at university (Bourelle 2009). While these courses can involve the construction, delivery and criticism of argumentation, they require little awareness of classical rhetorical theory and do not include the study of Latin or Greek literature or language (Murphy 2012). In cases where an advanced course of study in rhetoric is offered, this tends to incorporate logical reasoning and critical thinking (Turner 1998, Kugelmass 2008) rather than the study of rhetorical techniques or the delivery of speeches (Crowley and Hawhee 2012).

Essentially, the American rhetorical model is exclusively concerned with writing. We consider rhetoric to be of value in the improvement of writing skills, but we think that it also contributes to literacy, which also involves reading, speaking and listening. The optimal approach to rhetoric is one which allows learners to both construct and deconstruct communication and critically analyse theories of discourse, composition, and argumentation. This model of rhetorical pedagogy was the norm in the classical world but has become fragmented in contemporary conditions. In the following sections, we show how the rhetorical theories of Aristotle, Cicero and Quintilian are valuable not only for the learning and teaching of rhetoric but also for the preparation of citizens for democracy. In the classical world, rhetorical ability was inextricably linked with citizenship; rhetoric today has the potential to boost political literacy and help learners to understand how language choices 'form character and make good citizens' (Neel 1988: 211).

What is rhetoric, and where did it come from?

This section sets out the significance and complexity of what is meant by 'rhetoric' by tracing its origins in the classical period and examining its role in education and society in the Greek and Roman worlds. Almost since its inception, the nature, meaning and purpose of rhetoric have been contested. Current definitions of rhetoric include the practice of oratory; the study of strategies for effective oratory; the use of language, written or spoken, to inform or persuade; the study of the relation between language and knowledge; and the capacity to persuade others (Bizzell and Herzberg 1990). We consider all these definitions to be related to rhetoric, but do not think that it is possible, or desirable, to attempt to distil such a complex and contested concept into a single definition.

The Roman lawyer and statesman Cicero (*de Oratore* 3.2) explained that rhetoric requires eloquence but that it goes beyond the capacity to communicate effectively to encompass the power of persuasion. Classical rhetorical theory is a sensitive and complex theory of language which, from its inception, sought to demarcate and describe the operation of language in human affairs but at no point did it claim to include within its scope 'virtually all forms of discourse and symbolic communication' (Bizzell and Herzberg 1990: 2). Weaver *et al.* (1970) think that rhetoric is synonymous with communication and that rhetoric is necessarily present when one person addresses another. We disagree.

Of primary importance is the tension which exists between rhetoric as effective discourse and rhetoric as persuasive discourse. At the crux of this tension is the intention of the orator and the extent to which, in aiming to persuade, self-interest or the public good act as motivators. If rhetoric is viewed as a system of effective and articulate self-representation, it need not involve 'the use of empty promises and half-truths' (Bizzell and Herzberg 1990: 1) nor should it be linked to vacuous and malevolent verbal entrapment, 'excessive subtlety, manipulation and deceit' (Pernot 2005: 44). These slights are indicative of the widespread mistrust of rhetoric which has influenced its public perception from the classical world to this day. We contend that this negative view of rhetoric is erroneous: communication itself is neither admirable nor deplorable; rather that it is the intention and moral standing of the speaker and the willingness of the audience to be persuaded which influence such value judgements.

Rhetoric is a very particular form of communication which selects, from the vast realm of human discourse, occasions for speaking and writing that can be regarded as persuasive in intent. In this chapter, we identify the key areas of contestation which underpin and inform the claims and argumentation in subsequent chapters. In order to illuminate these areas of contestation, we interrogate the theories of key classical thinkers: Plato, Aristotle, Cicero and Quintilian. To adequately introduce their positions, it is necessary to provide details of their context, which will involve sketching related areas of rhetorical theory, including the relationship between philosophy and rhetoric, genres of rhetoric and parts of speech, the Roman reinterpretation of Greek rhetoric, the role of rhetoric in classical education and the conception of the ideal orator. It is on this broad explanatory foundation that the claims and argumentation in later chapters will be built. In concluding this chapter, we link the art of rhetoric with the way in which knowledge is created by argument and the way in which ideology and power are extended through discourse. This leads to discussion in Chapter 4 of the relationship between rhetoric and critical skills.

Origins of rhetoric in classical Greece

Until the fifth century BCE, Greece was ruled by tyrants, and there was little need for self-representation. For the ordinary citizen, prestige and reputation were measured in military prowess, the currency of success from the heroes of Homer's epic poems to the veterans of the Peloponnesian wars. Stories were transmitted orally, and speeches were delivered by oligarchs and plutocrats without concern for structure or style; their power ensured the desired outcome, so there was no need for persuasion. However, in 476 BCE Thrasybulus, the tyrant of Syracuse, was overthrown, and a democracy was formed. Under this despot, the land and property of many common citizens had been seized. For the first time, these ordinary people flooded the courts in an attempt to recover their property through oral self-representation. A certain Corax (about whom very little is known) devised an art of rhetoric which comprised simple techniques for effective presentation and argumentation in the law courts and permitted ordinary men to make their cases in public (Aristotle, *Rhetoric* 2, 24). His chief contribution was in helping to structure judicial speeches into various parts: prose, narration, statement of arguments, refutation of opposing arguments and summary. This structure serves as the basis for later rhetorical theories.

Rhetoric thereafter became 'a major cultural force' (Bizzell and Herzberg 1990: 20) in the golden age of Pericles (480–404 BCE) and was closely tied to the development of new forms of government and social organisation (Bizzell and Herzberg 1990: 20). In democratic Athens, generals took their orders from the assembly, which reached decisions after listening to the arguments on both sides (Thucydides acknowledged the importance of oratory by including speeches of this sort in his history of the Peloponnesian war [Book 2]); thus it was of prime civic importance (and often a matter of war or peace, death or life) for men to be able to express their views eloquently and articulately and to persuade their peers. Rhetoric quickly became an attractive subject of study, and men inspired by the rhetorical structure created by Corax began to travel around Greece teaching others how to represent their interests in public. These teachers were known as Sophists (wise men), and over time they devised their own conception of rhetoric, which they taught to those who could afford their fees. The Sophists should not be seen as 'populist-minded teachers' (Poulakos 1987: 101) wishing to educate the masses and bring succour to the hitherto voiceless and marginalised. Rather, their motivation for teaching rhetoric was to impart the secrets of effective persuasive argumentation for personal financial gain (Plato, *Hippias Maior*, 282c-d, Tell 2009).

The Sophistic conception of rhetoric, then, aware of the need for their paying customers to be successful in persuading others, attended increasingly to devising persuasive techniques rather than to constructing logical arguments. Thus, the Sophists are accused of reframing the rhetorical theory pioneered by Corax, moving it away from a framework in which arguments are most articulately phrased to the emotional and psychological manipulation of the audience. This shift from rhetoric being used as an honest and ethical method of self-representation to one which facilitated success, regardless of the pursuit of truth, attracted early criticism. Gorgias, one of the few Sophists for whom we have literary evidence, is vilified by the historian Diodorus (*Biblioteca historica* 12.135) for abusing rhetoric by employing naively exaggerated effects and laboured constructions which seemed ridiculous and excessively contrived in order to persuade his audience. Evidence survives, too, of Socrates' dialogue with Gorgias, and it is in this, and other works of Plato, that we find a battle line drawn between rhetoric and philosophy. Plato views both the Sophists and rhetoric as being dishonest, unethical and unscrupulous; this area of contestation warrants further consideration.

Plato

Plato recorded two dialogues between his teacher, Socrates,[1] and the Sophists, *Gorgias* and *Protagoras*. For Plato, rhetoric is the producer of persuasion (*Gorgias* 453a). He treats persuasion as a matter of deception and questions the possibility of ethical communication altogether. While in *Protagoras*, it appears that he viewed rhetoric as 'making the weaker account the stronger' as a method of improving a person's or city's objective condition (Schiappa 1999: 54). He identifies two types of rhetoric: common rhetoric and true rhetoric (*Gorgias* 517a). Common rhetoric is the misuse of rhetoric (*Gorgias* 457a1–2) commonly associated with the egotistical and profit-driven Sophists and their clients. True rhetoric has little in common with what people normally call rhetoric: it goes beyond ordinary rhetoric to the realm of philosophy. It is really a science used in the service of justice (*Gorgias* 527c) and the discourse of the philosopher (Pernot 2005: 51). Plato's philosophical conception of rhetorical theory can be distinguished from Sophistic rhetorical theory by its commitment to truth, even when truth conflicts with personal success (Schiappa 1999: 10). In exposing this tension between common and true rhetoric, Plato makes a clear distinction between the rhetorical life, which consists in looking for material success for oneself and for others and the philosophical life, which is directed towards the good and consists of taking care of one's soul and educating one's fellow citizens, whatever the cost to oneself (*Hippias Major* 304a–b, *Theaetetus* 172c).

This raises questions concerning responsible citizenship and the extent to which citizens communicate as a result of selfish or selfless motivations: deeper analysis of the contested conceptions of citizenship is presented in Chapters 2 and 3, and an attempt is made to reconcile rhetoric with democratic deliberation despite the tensions surrounding self-representation, self-interest and truth. The relationship between citizens, politics and communication is fundamental to this discussion, and it must be remembered that Plato's criticism of rhetoric is undoubtedly influenced by his contempt for democracy as a political model. For Plato, common rhetoric is the expression of a perverted way of seeing politics and as an adversary of democracy, he can only denounce[2] the art of oratory which was one of the mainsprings of this type of government (Pernot 2005: 46). Plato's damning criticism concludes that rhetoric is not an art, but an imitation of an art, in that it does not rest upon a true knowledge of its object (*Gorgias* 462c).

Aristotle

Aristotle, a pupil at Plato's Academy, however, claimed that rhetoric was an art but one of a special character (*Rhetoric* 1.1). He denied that rhetoric was a science with its own subject matter, but was rather a discipline unconcerned with the truth of its own conclusions. Aristotle saw rhetoric not as the art of persuading but rather the faculty of 'finding out in each case the existing means of persuasion' (*Rhetoric* 1.1355b25–26). It is in this distinction that Aristotle's view differs most from Plato's. Whereas for Plato, rhetoric was seen as a powerful force which promised easy victory over victims to be subjugated, Aristotle held that rhetoric was useful for bringing the truth to light, since some people could not be convinced by facts. If it is right to defend oneself by force, he thought it right to be able to do the same by words. His treatise introduces technical categorisation of rhetoric including the division of speeches into four parts (the introduction, the statement of the issue, the argument and the conclusion [Aristotle, *Rhetoric* 3.13]) and identifies the means for rhetorical discovery by analysing everything conducive to persuasion (Pernot 2005: 42). He admits that the power of words can be misused but contends that so can all good things (*Rhetoric* 1.1.1355b).

Whereas Plato favoured dialectic (the method of argumentation used by two or more people holding different points of view about a subject, who wish to establish the truth of the matter by dialogue with reasoned arguments), Aristotle saw it as a practice fraught with difficulty, typically marked by frustration rather than ease of achievement (*Topics,* Wardy 1996). Aristotle clarified the relationship between dialectic and rhetoric: whereas dialectic is persuasive discourse exclusively based on *logos* (logical argument), rhetorical persuasion also relies on *ethos* (credibility or character of the speaker) and *pathos* (emotional connection with the audience), irrational elements of communication which improve the relationship between the speaker and the audience (*Rhetoric* 1, 2). We argue in Chapters 3 and 4, following Aristotle, that rhetoric is a compound discipline in which a dialectical component is supplemented by knowledge of how to arouse, or appeal to, an audience's emotions and influence their impressions of a speaker's character. Aristotle's ideal orator knows the cognitive competencies and pertinent mental associations of those listening to him[3] and is ready to exploit forces already present in the listener. He builds on pre-existing ideas and recognised values, and in this way, he can effect the mystery of persuasion: to induce someone to think something they were not thinking before by introducing a new thought into the mind of the listener from known and accepted premises. This aspect of Aristotelian rhetorical theory is of central significance to our claim that rhetoric can help cultivate narrative imagination and empathy in learners, which will be subjected to rigorous analysis in Chapters 3 and 5. Aristotle's conclusion that rhetoric can act as an aid to reaching agreement on questions demanding immediate action in everyday life points to the deliberative function of rhetoric.

Roman reinterpretation of rhetoric

Cicero

Indeed, the political system at Rome under the Republic was highly conducive to the practice of deliberative rhetoric, a system of communication inherited from the Greeks. Whereas Aristotle's conception of deliberation was exercised among wealthy and educated Greek citizens, the Roman Republic presented the orator with a number of fora in which to utilise rhetoric for deliberative purposes. The Senate, open only to elected representatives from Italy's political and military elite, provided a discursive space in which views on political questions could be expressed orally by members of the body of elders and the consensus, once agreed, would be acted upon by elected magistrates. Unlike modern political assemblies, senators had not necessarily decided in advance which way they would vote, and so the debates were real: powerful speakers, regardless of their position in the hierarchy, had the chance of influencing the outcome (Clarke 1996: x). However, orators also had to be able to address a much larger, more diverse crowd in the form of the *contio*, Rome's public assembly open to all inhabitants regardless of social, political or economic status. Understandably, the art of deliberative rhetoric had to develop in order to accommodate the diverse needs of these multiple audiences since the content, style and tone of the orator's speech before the Senate and the *contio* would have to be quite different, as Cicero explains.

> And these ends can be achieved with less apparatus in the Senate, as that is a wise deliberative body, and one should leave room for many others to speak, besides avoiding any suspicion of a display of talent, whereas a public meeting (*contio*) permits of the full employment of powerful and weighty oratory and required variety.... But as the orator's chief stage seems to be the platform at a public meeting, it naturally results that we are stimulated to employ the more ornate kind of oratory.
>
> (Cicero, *de Oratore* 3.333-34, 338)

This quote, written by the foremost orator of the Roman Republic, indicates that within deliberative rhetoric, the Romans developed a scheme which regulated the different levels of language which an orator could employ depending on his audience. These included embellished style (*ornate*), fitting style (*apte*) and modest style (*decore*). In choosing which style to adopt, the orator had to exercise his critical faculties and identify with the mood and sympathies of his audience. In a development of the Aristotelian concept of the orator's *pathos*, we argue in Chapter 4 that the learning of rhetoric helps cultivate critical faculties. As Cicero held, communicators must make judgements about their audience in order to demonstrate awareness of their needs, thereby maximising their persuasiveness. Cicero himself is most famed for his use of the Asiatic style (*Brutus* 95, 325) in forensic oratory, which left juries stunned and captivated by his use of ornate and embellished language, delivered with dramatic and emotional flourish. It is this style of communication which has the greatest potential to seduce those unfamiliar with the rhetorical theory, and it is for this reason that we consider it vital for learners to become familiar with rhetoric so that they can deconstruct all the types of communication with which they are bombarded in today's world. Cicero's publications on rhetoric have provided a rich resource for rhetorical theorists for two centuries and the works of particular relevance to the argument expounded in this book are: *de Inventione* (a handbook for orators on how to best structure speeches), *de Oratore* (a fuller statement of rhetorical principles in dialogue form), *Topics* (a rhetorical treatment of common topics) and *Brutus* (a discussion of famous orators). In *de Inventione* (Book 3), for example, Cicero expands on Corax's and Aristotle's technical categorisation of rhetoric by delineating the parts of a speech (*partes orationis*)[4] in order to ensure effective and persuasive communication. Cicero's rhetorical works provide a window into the interpretation and reinterpretation of the Aristotelian rules of the genre and demonstrate how, for Cicero in the Roman Republic, rhetoric was more than persuasive discourse. It had a role to play in defending civic institutions. Setting forth the rules of rhetoric amounted to considering the conditions for the healthy functioning of the State (Pernot 2005: 114), and it is on this conception of rhetoric as a mainstay of civilisation that we build in Chapters 4 and 5. It was with the belief that rhetoric was a civic virtue that the first-century CE educator Quintilian placed it at the centre of the liberal arts curriculum in his school.

In addition to Aristotle's focus on ethos, pathos and logos, the 'rhetorical method', taught by Quintilian in his school, included the five canons of speech:

inventio (invention/discovery of arguments)

dispositio (arrangement/organisation of arguments/'brainstorming' content)

elocutio (style/word choice)

memoria (memorisation, reading from notes was not advised) and

actio (delivery/performance)

Cicero proposed that speeches should follow the following structure, taking full account of the five canons of speech:

- ***Exordium***, the opening in which the writer/speaker uses relevant generalities, anecdotes, quotes or analogies to capture listeners' attention and then connects them to the specific topic
- ***Narratio***, in which the author succinctly states what they will argue, stating which point is to be proven
- ***Divisio***, in which the author delineates the main points, reviews the debate and highlights specific topics to be discussed further
- ***Confirmatio***, which sets out the arguments for the proposition and provides evidence in support of them, usually employing a wide range of rhetorical techniques
- ***Refutatio***, which engages with the opposite view, refuting the counter-arguments
- ***Conclusio***, a summary of the argument, rousing listeners to agree

As can be seen from these ancient frameworks, the choosing of rhetorical techniques is governed by *elocutio*, and the orator must choose whichever techniques fit the content and mode of delivery. For example, the *exordium* (opening) might begin with an exclamation or a paradox in an effort to engage listeners' attention. The *confirmatio* (proof) might use a metaphor or rhyme to keep the audience's senses aroused. The *conclusio* (flourishing finish) might employ balanced phrasing, chiasmus or congeries verborum (a piling up of words). These techniques are still used by speechwriters (amateur and professional) today (Lancaster 2022, Szuplat 2024).

Quintilian and rhetorical education

Quintilian's aim was to produce the good man speaking well, one who combined a Platonic commitment to virtue and absolute truth with the Ciceronian focus on effective public service (Bizzell and Herzberg 1990: 35). Quintilian's ideal orator had to marry mastery of the art of rhetoric with oratorical competence and embody the moral conviction and social quality of someone who was devoted to the traditional institutions and values of Rome (Pernot 2005: 96). He was the sort of man the people could trust. According to the Roman historian Tacitus, gaining the trust of the nation was vital, as it led to success.

> The more able a man was at speaking, the greater the ease with which he attained high office and the greater his pre-eminence among his colleagues in office; he obtained more influence with the powerful, carried more weight with the Senate, possessed a higher reputation with the people.
>
> (Tacitus, *Dialogus* 36.4)

In gaining the trust of the audience, Quintilian advised that the orator was required to speak with careful consideration. Rhetoric was a route to social mobility there are several examples of young men climbing the social ranks as a result of their persuasive ability. Cicero is perhaps the best of such examples. In an extension of the Aristotelian conception of *ethos*, which held that orators were listened to not for their words in themselves but for their position in the city, Quintilian introduced additional essential elements to rhetorical discourse, including the orator's weightiness (*gravitas*) and his personal authority (*auctoritas*). *Auctoritas*, an 'elusive but vital mix of personal impressiveness and charisma with influence and connections' (Steel 2001: 13), played an important role in elevating the speaker's words and persuading his audience, as did his trustworthiness, forcefulness and brevity. The effectiveness of the orator, then, did not depend solely on the quality of the oratory.

This introduces another area of contestation: what is more important, true knowledge of the subject being discussed or the ability to deliver an effective speech, informed by rhetorical theory? For Quintilian, true knowledge of the topic under discussion was a prerequisite for the orator to successfully persuade, otherwise he would be a fraud. This view echoes Plato's, that it is most important for the orator to know the subject, to know it accurately for what it is, and to tell the truth. Under these circumstances, Plato thought that the plan of the oration would follow naturally from the subject itself, and the words would take care of themselves (Pernot 2005: 50). Aristotle is less concerned with the communication of truth, but rather that the orator speaks to make political and social life function on solid legal and moral foundations (Pernot 2005: 116). Pernot (2005: 115) summarises this area of contestation well:

> The question is one of knowing whether rhetoric is a technique without content, a collection of recipes applicable at will to any topic or if it is a complete art – putting into play all a person's qualities, supposing wisdom and knowledge in its expression and exercising its ability to persuade because of its inherent value.

The extent to which Cicero believed that the orator had to have strong moral conviction is unclear. Stroh (1975) and Steel (2001) identify instances where Cicero manipulates facts in his forensic speeches to produce a persuasively distorted account of events. Cicero has Crassus state (*de Oratore* 2) that 'no one can be eloquent about anything of which he is ignorant', but this statement is conjoined with the denial that 'no one can speak eloquently about the very thing he knows, even if his knowledge is perfect, if he is ignorant of how to make and polish an oration' (Wardy 1996: 101). Thus, for an orator to be successful, Cicero held that eloquence, knowledge of the subject and familiarity with rhetorical rules must be intertwined. In Chapter 3, we propose a slightly revised conception of rhetoric which accommodates the use of rhetoric in deliberative conversation in contrast to Cicero's conception, which limits rhetoric to monological performance in public.

Because rhetoric and oratory were to the fore in public arenas and were instrumental in the execution of Roman laws, politics, literature, philosophy and religion, knowledge of the rhetorical framework and the ability to apply it became a high priority in post-elementary education. Indeed, Benson and Prosser (1972: vii) claim that 'rhetoric played the central role in ancient education'. Once Roman boys had learned arithmetic, reading and writing (which included an emphasis on the study of grammar as this was regarded an important prerequisite to the acquisition of the elaborate declamatory style [Bizzell and Herzberg 1990: 34]), they hurried off to rhetorical schools such as the one run by Quintilian, to be taught how to speak and to argue. Indeed, Quintilian produced the first codified textbook on the theory and practice of rhetoric, the *Instituto Oratoria*, which is divided into theoretical, educational and practical constructs. A rhetorician, by the end of his training, should have been able to tell a story, defend a case, make a display or engage in argumentative dialectic (Wardy 1996: 103). At times during the early Republic, teachers of rhetoric and rhetorical schools were treated with suspicion.[5] This was perhaps because Roman aristocrats sought to limit the power and influence of 'new men' who did not descend from aristocratic families and so would not have experienced rhetorical training. Naïvely, it was believed that if these new men could not find teachers to train them in how to speak and argue well, they would be paralysed into inaction. Unsurprisingly, this intervention did not displace rhetoric from the school curriculum for long and, despite the 'evolutions of institutions and the vicissitudes of history' (Pernot 2005: 87), the study of rhetoric continued to include the study of Greek and Latin grammar, classical literature and history, logic and the composition and delivery of speeches. There was a virtual equation of an enlightened education with rhetorical training and in the evolving civic dynamic from Republic to Empire, rhetoric had changed from being primarily a political weapon to being the principal ingredient in Roman education and cultural life, a position it held 'until the end of antiquity' (Clarke 1996: xiii).

In many ways, the opposition of Plato to rhetoric, summarised in this chapter, is just as important as the support of Aristotle, Cicero and Quintilian: it is from the intricate, complex and tangled web of contested meanings that a revised conception of rhetoric will, we hope, rise like the proverbial 'phoenix from the ashes'. This chapter did not set out to define rhetoric; it has, however, given some indication of the multiple and, at times, divergent interpretations of the term from thinkers in the classical world to educators in the present day. As a first step in stimulating such a rebirth, we focus on its contribution to citizenship education and the cultivation of 21st century skills (Holmes-Henderson and Tempest 2018).

Notes

1 We cannot be sure how accurately Plato recorded the words of Socrates (Bonazzi et al. 2009) nor the extent to which the views expressed by Socrates in the dialogues have been influenced by Plato's own philosophical stance. Throughout, we conflate Socrates' position with that of Plato.

2 However, Plato included the study of rhetoric in the curriculum of his Academy because his aim was to prepare civic leaders (Bizzell and Herzberg 1990: 25), and he felt that it was important for potential political figures to understand ways in which they could best engage and address their fellow citizens.

3 Aristotle's orator is male because only men in ancient Athens were permitted to participate in public affairs. Hereafter, we use the masculine pronoun in cases where we refer to the classical conception (Greek and Roman) of the orator. A gender-neutral pronoun will be used later when referring to modern conceptions of the orator.

4 These are the *exordium* or opening, the *narratio* or statement of facts, the *divisio* or *partitio*, the statement of the point at issue and exposition of what the orator proposes to prove, the *confirmatio* or exposition of arguments, the *refutatio* or refutation of the opponent's arguments and finally the *conclusio* or peroration.

5 In 161 BCE, a decree of the Senate expelled philosophers and rhetoricians from Rome. Again in 92 BCE, Crassus, as censor, issued an edict with his colleague forbidding schools of rhetoric.

2 Rhetoric for citizenship

Minimal and maximal conceptions of citizenship

McLaughlin (1992: 236) identifies that 'much of the ambiguity and tension contained within the concept of citizenship can be roughly mapped in terms of minimal and maximal interpretations of the notion'. McLaughlin's distinction is useful because it allows multiple interpretations of citizenship to be viewed as part of a continuum rather than as discrete theories (McLaughlin 1992: 236). Since all conceptions of citizenship exist within a fluid civic domain inhabited by divergent political beliefs and are set against the contested nature of democracy itself, the continuum facilitates a method of philosophical analysis which eschews precise definition and fixed classification.

Four features of citizenship which McLaughlin identifies to illustrate the difference between minimal and maximal interpretations are: identity, virtues, political involvement and social prerequisites. In terms of identity, a minimal interpretation of citizenship centres on the legal status granted to a citizen. A maximal interpretation sees identity manifest itself as the conscious membership of a community and a shared commitment to democratic culture. In this sense, identity 'is dynamic rather than static in that it is seen as a matter for continuing debate and redefinition' (McLaughlin 1992: 236). The virtues required by a citizen within a minimal conception are primarily local and immediate in character. This might involve helping others through the demonstration of public-spiritedness, for example, by participating in a neighbourhood watch initiative, picking up litter or offering a seat on public transport to an older citizen. Interpreted maximally, the citizen has a responsibility to seek social justice for all. In a minimal interpretation of citizenship, political involvement extends only to the exercise of individual voting rights, whereas the maximal interpretation requires full participation in democracy. Social prerequisites concern the extent to which citizenship is seen as an 'egalitarian status in terms of theory and intention' (McLaughlin 1992: 237) in which case a minimal interpretation is content that citizenship is granted and a maximal one

DOI: 10.4324/9781003409069-3

is concerned that social disadvantages of various kinds must be considered if that status is to be achieved 'in any real and meaningful sense' (McLaughlin 1992: 237).

Education for citizenship

In the UK, over the last fifty years, there has been renewed interest in education for citizenship. A Citizenship Advisory Group was established in the 1990s (chaired by Professor Bernard Crick) to articulate the contemporary meaning of citizenship, drawing on philosophical ideas dating back to ancient Athens but essentially focussing on modern democracy. The National Curriculum Council concluded that 'education for citizenship is essential for every young pupil' (Jones and Jones 1992: 30) and in the Crick Report (Crick 1998), citizenship was recommended as a separate subject on England's national curriculum. The Curriculum and Assessment Review in England (Francis, 2025b) recommended greater focus on Citizenship education, particularly for children in primary schools. What skills will citizens need beyond school to thrive in society?

The next section considers twenty first-century skills.

Knowledge, understanding and twenty-first-century skills

Despite the increasing focus and attention, there is still no single or widely accepted definition of twenty-first-century skills. This is the result of multifarious agendas held by diversely positioned stakeholders in schools, universities, government departments and British businesses (for a detailed literature review, (see Suto, 2013). However, twenty-first-century skills can be broadly conceived as the core competencies which young people need to cultivate at school in order to succeed in life, learning and work.

Four government departments in England (the Department for Education, the Treasury, the Department for Trade and Industry and the Department for Work and Pensions) joined forces and produced a twenty-first-century skills strategy which sought to 'transform the economy and society' (Department for Education, 2003: 9) by refocusing the school curriculum on skill development. Since then, twenty-first-century skills have been afforded increasing importance in educational policy and curriculum design. Skills England was established in 2025 to lead on this agenda, and to ensure that skills needed for economic growth are prioritised in education and training. We give a summary of the skills which regularly appear in the list of priorities for global school curricula:

Learning and thinking skills

- Critical thinking
- Creative thinking
- Collaborating
- Communicating

Literacy skills

- Functional literacy
- Information literacy
- Media literacy
- Digital literacy

Life skills

- Flexibility
- Initiative
- Social skills
- Productivity
- Leadership

What does the study of rhetoric contribute to the cultivation of twenty first-century skills? As we shall see in Part B, there are a number of ways in which the study of rhetoric can help cultivate initiative, productivity and leadership; indeed, the very experience of a broad and balanced curriculum has long been recognised as providing 'life skills' (especially social skills and flexibility) which school leavers need to succeed in the world of work. We are currently operating in a climate where educational settings need to make skills development more explicit. We need to make sure we integrate the development and awareness of the skills students are acquiring without diluting the substance of learning experiences. The aim is not to suggest that a focus on employment should drive course and assessment design – far from it. More simply, we share examples of how we can help students understand and enhance the skills with which the study of rhetoric already provides them, as well as how we might update these for the unpredictable demands of the future job market. How might these skills complement AI, or help employees to do something which AI cannot?

Rhetoric can develop learning and thinking skills such as critical thinking and communication, as well as making a significant and positive impact on learners' literacy skills; the case studies in Chapter 6 provide evidence for, and illuminate, these claims.

Critical reasoning

Citizens become critical when they possess the skills to analyse alternative beliefs and can articulate and defend their views in a way which shows respect for others and an awareness of democracy and social justice. The focus on the individual amassing knowledge in order to understand alternative social and cultural approaches is undoubtedly one stage in the process. Indeed, knowledge and understanding are closely linked with the aims of international education and the development of global citizens. Knowledge and understanding certainly have a preparatory role to play, but they stop short of improving students' sense of agency or advancing their competence in political literacy, elements which we consider necessary to move beyond a basic conception of citizenship. The absence of any explicit mention of shared commitment to public virtues and social justice, combined with the focus on the individual's knowledge and understanding, aligns with a minimal interpretation of citizenship; McLaughlin suggests that such conceptions do not have any 'concern to ameliorate the social disadvantages that may inhibit the students from developing into citizens in a significant sense' (McLaughlin 1992: 238). The danger of a minimal interpretation of this kind being taught in schools is that it can lead students to receive 'merely an unreflective socialisation into the political and social status quo' (McLaughlin 1992: 238), which is insufficient for contemporary education and society.

At this stage, it is helpful to remember that citizenship, according to McLaughlin, should not be considered as a set of distinct concepts but is better viewed as a 'continuum of interpretations' in which minimal conceptions are no less concerned with 'ideological content or significance' (McLaughlin 1992: 237) than their maximal counterparts. Rather, the main difference concerns the degree of critical understanding and questioning that is seen as necessary for citizenship. Rhetoric has much to offer the teaching of citizenship: pupils learn how to interrogate beliefs, critically examine evidence and apply reason.

The connection between responsible citizenship and 'leading the examined life' has long been considered strong (discussed in Plato's *Apology*, Aristotle's *Politics*, St. Augustine's *Confessions* and Descartes' *Meditations*), but to what extent should citizens be allowed to choose the extent to which they participate in democratic processes? Any demand that citizens participate or engage in critical reason is 'to go beyond the demands of liberal neutrality' (Galston 1989: 100 in McLaughlin 1992: 241). Freedom, Galston maintains, 'entails the right to live the unexamined life as well as examined lives' so public education ought not to induct citizens into the belief that critical reason is an essential skill for citizenship. This view is characteristic of the extremely minimal end of the continuum of citizenship. Where does the challenge from democratic autonomy leave critical reasoning and rhetoric for citizenship?

This tension is eased if the curriculum is viewed as the vehicle through which citizens learn the skills and knowledge they require to reason and participate in society, and if they retain the choice to exert these skills fully, partially or not at all at various stages throughout their lives. To preserve democratic autonomy, there ought to be no compulsion to reason critically, yet we consider it vital for young citizens to learn the skills required for critical reasoning, whether they then choose to apply them immediately and extensively or not. A sensible location for these skills to be developed is school.

Active and participatory citizenship

The commitment to participate becomes connected with 'active citizenship'. Active citizenship denotes moving beyond personal responsibility to active participation in which critical reasoning and collaboration with others are required.

As Kymlicka and Norman argue (1994: 361), 'emphasising participation does not yet ensure that citizens participate responsibly – that is, in a public-spirited, rather than self-interested or prejudiced way'. In fact, citizens who choose to participate vociferously in public might do so for their own gain, at the expense of 'less powerful groups whose needs are greater' (Enslin and White 2003: 122). Central to the conception of active citizenship is the need for learners to make choices which are informed by their critical faculties and which conform to ethical and responsible standards of conduct. This challenge to participatory citizenship can be defused by stressing commitment to morality and virtues beyond the local, which is required by maximal conceptions of citizenship. The act of participation is neither virtuous nor base by nature, rather it is the intention of the participant which is of primary significance in determining its morality. In the context of a pluralistic democracy, what is required is the concrete specification of which public virtues ought to be upheld. This represents an opportunity for the exercise of active citizenship.

Active citizenship, then, requires a maximal interpretation of citizenship and, as reference to the critical literature attests, it goes beyond mere participation to demand a commitment to responsible participation informed by open and robust methods of democratic deliberation; 'engaging in debate, discussion and controversy and using skills of engaging with and arguing with alternative viewpoints' (Ross 2008: 69) 'in the search for possible answers' (Brown and Fairbrass 2009: 6). This commitment to participate in controversy and to deliberate with others is far removed from minimal interpretations of the capacity which stem from the focus on cultural knowledge, understanding and the possession of 'commitment to participate responsibly'. There are, however, some risks attached to active citizenship which make it potentially undemocratic and exclusive. These will now be examined.

Some interpretations of active citizenship limit qualifying acts to those performed in the public sphere. What about active citizenship in relation to activity done 'in the private realm by way of reproduction and care of dependents' (Enslin and White 2003: 119). This public conception of active citizenship poses the risk that activity done at home does not qualify as active and, consequently, those who actively participate in the private sphere are not seen as performing their civic duty and cannot be citizens 'at home – at least beyond a minimal sense of citizenship' (Enslin and White 2003: 119). We caution that such an approach has the potential to marginalise the participation of some citizens, and that the absence of a coherent approach to the inclusion of active citizenship on the policy agenda means that it remains open to minimal and maximal interpretation.

A maximal interpretation of active citizenship, though, offers exciting possibilities for an increased focus on political literacy and could accommodate increased awareness of the democratic dimensions of participation. Located 'predominantly at the social end of the spectrum' and lacking 'an explicit political and democratic dimension', Biesta (2008: 45) considers the personally responsible conception of citizenship to be inadequate for preparing citizens to participate in advancing democracy. A fundamental problem with the conception of the personally responsible citizen is that it is overly oriented to social life (e.g., giving to charity, volunteering and environmental projects) and is not sufficiently directed towards political participation. There is the danger that 'voluntarism and kindness are put forward as ways of avoiding politics and policy' leading to young people 'learning that citizenship does not require democratic governments, politics and even collective endeavours' (Westheimer and Kahne 2004: 243). We believe that young people need to feel empowered as political actors who have an understanding both of the opportunities and the limitations of individual political action, and who are aware that real change (affecting structures rather than simply operations within existing structures) often requires collective action through public and political initiatives.

The case for difficult citizenship and the role of rhetoric in its development

'Difficult' citizenship 'requires raising questions about the stories underlying geographic, political and historical phenomena, and thereby disrupting the repetition of comforting knowledges' (Bickmore 2008: 60). 'Disruption' and 'justice-oriented' citizenship represent a paradigm shift from the law-abiding, environmentally aware and charitable activity associated with personally responsible participation. In this maximal interpretation of citizenship, students are encouraged and empowered to take effective political action since this conception of citizenship calls explicit attention 'to matters of injustice and to the importance of pursuing social justice... by analysing and understanding the interplay of social, economic and political forces' (Westheimer and Kahne 2004: 242). This resonates with what was, for Crick, the essence of education for citizenship, that students should have an 'inquisitive turbulence about the manifold relationships of ideas to institutions' (Crick 2000: 15).

In contrast to the local priorities conceived within a minimal interpretation, citizenship construed maximally requires that activity is informed by the critical faculties and supported by an explicit understanding of democratic principles, values and procedures on the part of the citizen. This does not mean that students must, necessarily, be encouraged to start campaigns, protest or become warriors for social causes, but rather that they develop the ability to ask difficult questions and pursue solutions oriented to social justice within a political society. It is this empowering and transformative form of citizenship which we consider has the most to offer contemporary education and democracy, and which we ought to promote. Rhetoric has a unique and valuable role to play.

Rhetoric, critical reasoning and political involvement

Rhetoric, if utilised as a pedagogical tool, can boost critical literacy and increase political involvement. The rhetorical framework offers a route to democratic confidence for young citizens, in that it foregrounds a range of skills and competencies which equip them with germane skills vital for citizenship: the ability to deconstruct the communication of others and to construct communication which effectively expresses their views. It can act as a vehicle for effective self- expression and as a tool which facilitates active participation through the articulation of complex civic issues in a collaborative and deliberative manner. Empowering students to value their potential for positive action takes us one step closer to the 'disruption' encouraged by difficult citizenship.

Political involvement, interpreted maximally, requires participation, but as was indicated above, participation can be a problematic concept. Of particular interest here, is that participation does not necessarily demand that students consider and engage with issues beyond their immediate concerns and responsibilities. Rhetorical training involves reflection, articulation and deliberation. The use and development of critical skills to reflect on and articulate the reasoning behind participation not only validates the civic activity but also encourages students to think beyond their immediate rights and responsibilities. They come to consider what participation may be required of others (either individuals or institutions) to further the social or political cause. Rhetoric furnishes learners with skills to articulate the complexity of their active participation, a facet of citizenship education which we ought to promote in the hope that when they are asked to articulate and critique their participation in, for example, local problem-solving civic initiatives, students might come to realise that activity of this nature does not confer deeply transformative effects (Ross and Munn 2008) and that their efforts can have even greater impact.

The ability of individuals within society to hold and articulate different conceptions of the good life, different values and different ideas about what matters to them is essential for the functioning of a democratic society. Rhetoric can provide a common communicative framework for diversely positioned participants, equipping citizens with tools to articulate their dissent and reject any perceived homogeneity. This process of reflection, articulation and deliberation may, as a result, open up increased cognitive space for more detailed consideration of alternative conceptions of society and lead to a better understanding of, and commitment to, justice-oriented citizenship.

Young people need communicative competence to engage in cultural and community development and change (Deuchar 2003: 36). The maximal interpretation of citizenship education we promote extends beyond pedagogical approaches which privilege the transmission of knowledge and cultivation of personal responsibility, to focus on the cultivation of critical reasoning, self-expression and political participation.

According to Aristotle, to lead the good life and to fulfil our humanity, we must enter into the *polis* (city) as citizens and into political relationships with other citizens. He saw politics as an activity among free citizens which concerned how they governed themselves by public debate (Crick 2008: 16) as 'to be political and to live in a *polis* meant that everything was decided through words and persuasion and not through violence'(Arendt 1958: 26–27). Rhetoric, one method of operation for this communication, was so successful that it became a necessary skill for participation in ancient democracies, and there is much to be gained from revisiting the classical conception of citizenship, which was inextricably linked to critically informed oral participation. This focus on democracy, talking and citizenship will be pursued in more detail below. Now we consider how rhetoric can play an important role in preparing citizens for participation in democratic deliberation.

Public debate: rhetoric for democratic deliberation

According to Bohman (1998), Dryzek (2000), Chambers (2003) and others,[1] democratic theory has taken a 'deliberative turn' (Hansen 2012: 12). Deliberation is conceived of as a process in which arguments on both sides of a problem or issue are considered by members of the public who participate in decision-making on matters of relevance and importance to public life, as equals. It assumes that no one can determine beforehand what the right answer to the given political question is; and therefore, 'a *prima facie* duty exists to hear different viewpoints and to give them, and those who present them, the sort of respect we would ask for ourselves' (Bentley 2004: 115).

Deliberation offers citizens with opposing views the opportunity to explain and justify the foundations of their beliefs in an effort to transform the alternative opinions held by fellow deliberators and in so doing enable all sides to reach new and acceptable positions for collective action (McDonald 2012: 200). Importantly, participating in public deliberation of this sort can be seen as constituting citizenship (Asen 2004: 189) since individuals become citizens by discursively – and we suggest rhetorically – engaging one another collaboratively and critically in the public sphere. Having to articulate your position, listen to others, adjust your stance and formulate new views exercises the skills we have hitherto connected with the teaching and learning of rhetoric: literacy (particularly 'oracy' i.e. listening and speaking), critical literacy and critical thinking. In Athens, the practice of democracy was predicated on the assumption that citizens possessed the capacity to reason together, in public (as well as in private), and that the results of those deliberations would (in general and over time) conduce to the common good.

Composing, delivering, criticising and judging arguments are skills at the core of democratic deliberation and the exercise of these cross-curricular skills 'promotes democratic practice immediately' (Ivie 2002: 277) and provides an ideal opportunity for students to use their rhetorical knowledge for the purpose of civic participation. Following Young, we believe that rhetoric can give a voice to the traditionally underrepresented and marginalised groups in society, thereby improving equality and inclusion within deliberative democracy. The linguistic and analytical skills studied as part of rhetorical education contribute positively to the cultivation of competence and confidence in civic participation and the production of citizens who can critically assess the complex dimensions of democratic decision-making. Ober (2005: 130) reminds us that the legacy left to us by classical Greece has much to offer our contemporary understanding of deliberation: then, as now, deliberating 'meant listening as well as speaking; accepting good arguments as well as making them'.

Deliberative rhetoric

Aristotle, in addition to his definition of rhetoric ('the faculty of discovering the possible means of persuasion in reference to any subject whatever' [*Rhetoric* 1356a2]) wrote that the function of rhetoric is to 'deal with things about which we deliberate' (1357a12) and in the *Nicomachean Ethics*, he describes deliberation as a kind of excellence of thinking (1142b15) used when we deliberate about future things which are in our power, fluid, open to change and not fixed (1112b7). In *Politics* (1.1253a2), he claimed that we are political animals and, as such, our happiness as individuals depends to a great extent on what happens in our community. Young *et al.* (2010: 433) endorse Aristotle's conclusion that we are political animals and suggest that 'we must reframe politics as our job description'. In the classical Athenian conception of the *polis*, discursive engagement in civic life was inextricably linked to the duty of citizenship, and the process of democratic deliberation is one aspect of Athenian political life which we propose warrants reconsideration in the current climate. Aristotle claimed that the political community is centred around communication with each other concerning what we think is 'advantageous and harmful, and therefore just and unjust' (*Politics* 1253a3). Democratic deliberation necessarily involves speech and argument because it requires the sharing of our reasoning, and the means by which we communicate our reasoning to each other in public deliberation is the particular form of persuasive speech that Aristotle called deliberative rhetoric (*Rhetoric* 1.3.1358b5). Thus, for Aristotle, deliberation is a kind of argumentation or collective thinking in which a group is trying to decide on the best course of action in a situation requiring choice but also involving uncertainty. Deliberative rhetoric seeks to persuade us that one course of action rather than another will best serve the common good (*Rhetoric* 1351b). As such, it has two basic elements: some form of public reasoning, in which citizens exchange their views on matters of common interest; and an opportunity to consider together this exchange of opinions and arguments to reach decisions about which collective action to support. In the Greek model, deliberative rhetoric was integral to the political life of the *polis*; it was at the heart of everyday politics within the citizen body and was necessary for the improvement and advancement of civic life.

In demanding the construction, analysis and adaptation[2] of argument, Aristotle's conception of deliberative rhetoric could be viewed as a tool for communicative empowerment which has the potential to lead individuals and groups to action. For this reason, and given the worrying backdrop of widespread current civic disengagement (Dewey 1927, Putnam 2000, Putnam and Feldstein 2003, Hogan 2008, Nussbaum 2010, Biesta 2011) we turn to Dewey (1927: 208), who argued that the means of political learning lay in communication, 'the essential need', he wrote, 'is the improvement of the methods and conditions of debate, discussion and persuasion. That is the problem of the public'. In the new millennium, the USA is still trying to address this deficiency in its education system: Putnam (2000) lists many initiatives underway in the USA to improve civic engagement, replenish the nation's social capital and to rebuild deliberative communities. Surprisingly, however, Hogan (2008: 76) records that few of these efforts have emphasised the most fundamental requirement of a sustainable deliberative democracy: citizens with the communicative competencies needed to participate in civic life. If citizens are to participate competently and confidently, it is vital that they know how to articulate their own views and how to listen to others both in person and online.

The best answers to problems of political alienation and civic disengagement are to be found not in new information technologies, but in a revival of some of the oldest traditions in rhetorical theory and practice (Hogan 2008: 77).

We suggest that the teaching and learning of rhetoric is complementary to the successful enactment of democratic deliberation. There are, however, objections to this view from theorists who consider rhetoric unsuitable for deliberative purposes. We consider four of the most challenging objections to our claim that rhetoric contributes positively to democratic deliberation and now address these challenges from equality, emotions, self-interest and monology.

Notes

1 For example, McKerrow (1998), Hauser and Benoit-Barne (2002), Carpini et al. (2004), Fontana et al. (2004), Chambers (2009), Healy (2011) and Kock and Villadsen (2012).

2 By this, we mean the requirement to adapt content and delivery mid-speech in response to audience reaction.

3 Reasons not to teach rhetoric?

The challenge from equality

Norval (2007: 65), among others,[1] notes that arguments for equality are central to democratic deliberation as we must treat each other as equal partners, 'individuals must be given the space to speak, and we must listen to each other, and justify our positions to one another' (Norval 2007: 22). Historically, rhetoric, as a method of communication, has been considered unequal since in classical Greece only those who were free-born male citizens were permitted to participate in public discussions and in Rome rhetoric arguably became a tool of the elite to manipulate the commoners into voting a particular way in judicial and deliberative contexts. In both Greece and Rome, women, slaves and foreigners were voiceless; they had no political rights and were helpless to effect any change in their positions. Hence the restriction of rhetorical education and practice to learned men might be seen as a contributory factor to the ongoing suppression of already marginalised members of society. Modern criticisms of the use of rhetoric in deliberation object to these origins which seem undemocratic by modern standards and lambast its use by, largely, wealthy, well-educated, Caucasian men with a particular personal interest, these being found primarily among the politicians of developed Western nations. At a time when social mobility, widening participation and 'levelling up' are priorities in education, we must remain alert to the differences in context between ancient and modern. Donna Zuckerberg's book 'Not all dead white men' (2018) provides useful background here.

Of course this very book springs from our deep-seated belief that knowing and practising rhetoric is of value to all learners, regardless of their particular background, family circumstances or social class. How does rhetoric fit with argumentation and is there just one acceptable method of communication within deliberative contexts? If there are multiple methods, what value is added by the rhetorical framework? Aiming at persuasion and most effective in contentious environments, can rhetoric be reconciled with the democratic aims of deliberation and its commitment to equality of participation and influence? It is to these questions that we now turn.

DOI: 10.4324/9781003409069-4

Much of this relates to the equality of communication within schools, for example, school leaders' communication with staff and/or parents, discussion at school council or governors' meetings. Who gets to speak, and what power dynamics are at play which amplify some voices and silence others? This may manifest itself through specific operating models and decision-making processes related to staff, student or family communication content, for instance, led by senior teams. Policies might be compiled that are written by leaders and enacted by teachers, or indeed, co-constructed by working parties ahead of implementation in which case, multiple layers of staff workforce and the school community are represented. There might be school standards related to the delivery of lesson content, whereby a group of middle and senior leaders agree on a shared language that becomes a way to build familiarity and a sense of belonging across classrooms for students. These choices, designed to convey information in a way that holds clarity, also implicitly become a vehicle through which specific members of the school community make decisions regarding the formality, delivery and implications of communications.

Benhabib holds that there is just one accepted form of communication within deliberative democracy: critical argumentation (Benhabib 1996: 82). Her stance here echoes Habermas (1993: 163), who held that argumentation was 'the only truly legitimate mode of discursive communication as it renders the deliberative process rational and confers on it authority'. She defends this position by privileging the peculiar

> rhetorical structure of the rule of law and insisting that the moral ideal of impartiality is a regulative principle which should govern not only our deliberations in public but also the articulation of reasons by public institutions (Benhabib 1996: 83).

She suggests that without such a focussed approach to the equality and impartiality of communication, the open justification of opinions and the admission of reasons and motivations behind particular stances, neither the ideal of the rule of law nor reasoned deliberation can be sustained. Benhabib's position is contrary to that of Young (1997), who argues that such a restricted approach within deliberation is exclusionary. She considers that it attempts to homogenise and neutralise what differentiates us as participants in the deliberative process and hence negates the distinctive situated knowledge and understanding that diversely positioned participants can bring to the deliberative process (Benhabib 1996, Young 1997). Young advocates a move beyond deliberative democracy to what she terms 'communicative democracy' (Young 1997: 60), where the uniformity and impartiality of communication are abandoned in favour of a more inclusive model of communication which accommodates social and cultural difference.

Young justifies this position by highlighting that the 'norms of deliberation are culturally specific and often operate as forms of power that silence or devalue the speech of some people' (Young 1997: 63) and proposes 'three elements that a broader conception of communicative democracy requires in addition to critical argument: greeting, rhetoric and storytelling' (Young 1997: 69). These, she suggests, recognise the situated nature of the speakers and 'supplement argument by providing ways of speaking across difference in the absence of significant shared understandings' (Young 1997: 69). In promoting more inclusive methods of communication within communicative democracy, Young's selection of rhetoric is of particular interest. Whereas Benhabib discounts it from democratic deliberation because it moves people to action 'without having to render an account of the bases upon which it induces people to engage in certain courses of action rather than others' (Benhabib 1996: 83), Young recognises its positive capacity to 'get and keep attention' and to situate the 'speaker, audience, and occasion' (Young 1997: 71) which, she holds, serves a connecting function.[2]

If we lose rhetoric, as Benhabib suggests, we lose something important from citizen exchange and citizen education. Following Young, we hold that it is necessary to engage with and embrace difference when communicating with the 'other' within democracy. In an elaboration of Young's position, we defend rhetoric's capacity to reach 'the other' by focussing on the opportunity it presents to participants within deliberation for the cultivation of empathy and narrative imagination. Because the rhetorical framework presents a unified method of communication, deliberators are more likely to experience equality in representation, participation and influence. This position is motivated by our primary concern; what we teach in the classroom prepares students for life beyond, and, in this regard, we consider the purpose of democratic education to be to induct everybody into reasoned critical argument.

Rhetoric can minimise perplexity within deliberation, we propose, since it offers a communicative method which combines critical argumentation (Benhabib's chosen method) and some of the more inclusive elements Young suggests. In addition to critical argumentation, rhetoric promises an additional advantage which merits attention in response to Benhabib's rejection. By necessarily regarding, articulating and responding to the positions of 'the other', it enables a connection between speaker and audience which is enhanced by the consideration of emotions, narrative imagination and empathy. Whereas critical argumentation is associated with the production of appeals to reason and logic based on evidence about things known, rhetoric involves persuasive argumentation in conflictive environments where uncertainty abounds. Matters for discussion within democratic deliberation tend to involve disagreement regarding how best to proceed collectively when the eventual outcome is unknowable. Rhetoric, then, through its persuasive appeal to the emotions in reaching consensus,[3] is more suited to deliberation than critical argumentation alone, which presumes that one argument can be conclusive and final when the subject matter is unknown, a position which Aristotle thought was untenable (*Rhetoric* 1. 112b7).

Classical rhetorical theory represents another improvement on critical argumentation because the inclusion of *refutatio* (refutation of opponent's argument) requires that the speaker consider opposing positions and, after articulating them, respond to them in a critically informed way. In many cases, this involves the use of *ethopoeia*, a technique which requires orators to put themselves in the place of others and give a speech as that other character. The obligatory process of 'becoming the other' (Cicero, *de Inventione* 1.42–51, Quintilian, *Instituto Oratoria* 5.13), represents for contemporary deliberative democracy a valuable opportunity to engage with the thoughts and feelings of marginalised and oppositional groups and should lead to improved mutual understanding and respect between participants in deliberative settings. In this sense, rhetoric goes some way to cultivating narrative imagination,[4] compassion and empathy, which may contribute to the transformation of original position, which Young considered important to the discursive process (Young 1997: 68).

The transformative potential of rhetoric

That members of deliberative communities are diversely positioned is clear, and Benhabib's concept of 'egalitarian reciprocity' recognises that 'within discourses, each should have the same right to various speech acts, to initiate new topics and to ask for justification of the presuppositions of the moral conversation' (Benhabib 2002: 107). It is difficult, though, to balance such a notion of egalitarian reciprocity with her preference for critical argumentation as the uniform method of communication, as within critical argumentation there are bound to be variances in citizens' argumentative ability (if it can be learned through experience, we can foresee a general increase in ability over time). Diversity in individual experience can, in turn, contribute to the perception of authoritativeness in a deliberative forum, and we can reasonably see that members of the community with both more life experience and more argumentative ability will have a more robust sense of which speech acts are useful and which are incompatible with deliberative consensus. Critical argumentation can be taught through reference to logic, literacy and causality, but rhetoric offers a structured, defined and accessible framework, which provides a more cohesive, practical communicative solution, offering particular value to those whose voices are traditionally less represented within deliberative contexts.

Subverting the view that rhetoric is a tool for perpetuating inequality, Crowley and Hawhee (2012: 5) claim instead that it offers an avenue to 'rectifying power inequities among citizens'. In this regard, it can empower them 'to move from being governed to having agency' (Hauser 2008: 255) and can equip them with the capacity to negotiate across difference. Beyond the 'bonding' function of rhetoric outlined by Dryzek (2010: 327) (this concerns communication between people who are similar in social background, therefore not inclined to air differences and as a result associate only with those who agree with them), we consider that rhetoric can be viewed as a bridge 'between people with different social characteristics and backgrounds' (Dryzek 2010: 327) thereby improving the equality of opportunity to participate in discursive fora. A bridge is necessary because in deliberative democracy, conflict is inevitable. 'For a rhetorical democracy to flourish, controversies should be welcomed, encouraged, stimulated and even organised in order to implicate ordinary citizens in decision-making' (McDonald 2012: 201).

Conflicts among groups and classes permeate modern democratic societies and conflictive relationships represent the origin of rhetoric; they 'are the wellspring from which rhetorical practices flow' (Hauser 2008: 238). The rhetorical framework, then, can act as a bridge between those traditionally trapped in asymmetrical power relations to communicate using a uniform method: it represents an opportunity to link differently situated and differently disposed actors when they 'call into question the opinions of others... bring them into the light for examination and negotiation, and... listen to each other' (Crowley and Hawhee 2012: 5). Rhetorical education represents freedom from victimisation and the repositioning of those who have historically been unheard, as well as those whose early education, upbringing and cultural roots have discouraged active participation in civic life.

In time, this bridging function of rhetoric could have positive ramifications, including narrowing the gap in social cohesion and improving confidence and competence in civic engagement. Hauser (2008: 244) suggests that 'equity is essential to maintaining horizontal relations among citizens participating in a deliberative process that is more than nominally democratic' and rhetoric, because of the structured nature of the framework, widens access and grants equity to the contributions of all citizens in deliberative processes. Its contribution to understanding 'the other' and articulating their position necessarily involves critical engagement at an emotional level, generating empathy. However, there is also a danger here: speakers may inappropriately appeal to the emotions and passions of fellow citizens rather than their reason within deliberative democracy. Following Aristotle and Young, we suggest that the emotions play a vital role in civic decision-making. Therefore the centrality of emotionally persuasive appeals to rhetorical communication is positive both for reaching consensus in deliberative settings and for helping citizens to develop their critical faculties.

The challenge from the emotions

Within classical rhetorical theory, the orator can engage and employ his own emotions, and those of his audience, in three ways. First, there is the gauging of the audience's emotion by the orator, in which he considers how he might best align his words to successfully persuade his listeners to come to accept a specific claim. When an orator invents new arguments, he ought to begin the process within the citizens' opinions rather than outside them. Aristotle (*Rhetoric* 2.1) suggests, since through the study of the structure of people's characters and emotions, he could find deliberative pathways within which to best frame his arguments. Young considers rhetoric to be of benefit in this regard since it involves 'orienting one's claims and arguments to the particular assumptions, history, and idioms of [the] audience' (Young 2002: 65). Second, through the delivery of *ethopoeia* and *refutatio* the orator uses 'empathy to figure out what his audience is thinking about an issue, what they accept on the issue or can be brought to accept' (Walton 2004: 319) and begins to engage and stir up suitable emotions through his performance. We said above that speakers need to consider both the sympathetic and the dissenting voices within the communities in which they communicate; this improves their awareness of the 'other' within contemporary democratic deliberation. Successful public speakers, then, will generally have to measure the emotional temperature of their audience, incorporate corresponding sensitivity into their arguments and acknowledge that the audience's emotional position plays an important role in the argumentative process. Third, the final stage in the emotional process, the classical orator selects the appropriate level of language (e.g., embellished style [*ornate*], fitting [*apte*] or modest [*decore*]), shaping the speech to the audience's perceived emotional needs and displaying emotion himself, commensurate with his content and aims of his speech. Connolly urges that the appeal to, and display of, emotion ought not to be seen as 'extra seasoning' (Connolly 2007: 147), but rather a crucial step in the communication of ideas.

For Plato, this appeal to the audience's particular emotional needs was deceitful and rhetoric's propensity to delight and please the people's appetites made it nothing more than a form of flattery (*Gorgias* 463b) or manipulation which was incompatible with reason. The adaptation of oneself to the peculiarities and idiosyncrasies of an audience amounted to trickery and was inconsistent with the behaviour of a good citizen (*Gorgias* 503b). Thus rhetoric was, for Plato, a type of speech which he likened to the art of cooking; used to cater to, and to indulge, the undisciplined and restless appetites of the people (*Gorgias* 464b). It created the appearance of grace and pleasure in the conscious embellishments of speaking and performing by appealing to the senses, an appeal thought inappropriate for rational speech (*Gorgias* 472c). In Plato's view, the philosopher uses speech to instruct, and thus to improve the listener, aiming at what is best for them by appealing to reason which acts as the guide and ruler of the soul by 'disciplining the appetites and controlling the passions' (Fontana 2004: 42). Rhetoric, in contrast, he saw as a 'knack' (*Gorgias* 462c), 'a kind of influencing of the mind by means of words' (*Phaedrus* 261a) and he saw rhetoricians as men who 'steal away our souls with their embellished words' (*Menexenus* 235a); in this way, he despised the 'negative effect of rhetoric's persuasive appeals on the capacity of listeners to exercise rational judgement' (Shiffman 2004: 101).

Plato's concerns were shared by Kant, who also complained of rhetoric's incompatibility with reason. Conceiving of rhetoric as a dialectic which borrows from poetry only so much as is needed to win minds to the side of the orator before they have formed a judgement and to deprive them of their freedom (Kant 1951: 53. 172), he believed that rhetoric 'moved men like machines' (Kant 1951: 5. 328n). In contrast, reason 'is always simply the agreement of free citizens, of whom each one must be permitted to express without let or hindrance, his objections or even his veto' (Kant 2007, A738–739, B766–767). In this conception, the appeal to the emotions of the audience acts as a barrier to reason, hindering citizens' exercise of freedom.

The criticism of rhetoric by Plato and Kant, that it is irrational, anticipates more recent arguments by some advocates of deliberative democracy, who contend that true democracy is characterised by reasoned public discourse. Habermas stated that deliberations should be determined 'by the force of the better argument' so that participants in deliberation are 'required to state their reasons for advancing proposals, supporting them or criticising them' (McCarthy 1975: 108), a position which draws on Plato's condemnation of rhetoric for not explaining the reason anything happens, and is clearly the impetus for Benhabib's criticism[5] of rhetoric highlighted above. Certainly, the modern conception of democratic deliberation rests on the assumption that when a group of people get together to deliberate, if they weigh the relative merits of both sides of an issue thoughtfully and carefully, the conclusion they arrive at is reason-based and supported by objective evidence (Walton 2004: 303).

Hence democratic deliberation in current conditions becomes a rational basis for action. In the ancient world, however, deliberation was seen as representing an important framework of argumentation in its own right, including appeal to the passions and emotions to support a conclusion, and this represents an approach to deliberation which we think is worthy of reconsideration.

Aristotle argued that judgement about the possible courses of action presented in the public sphere ought not to exclude partiality and passion as, together with the emotions, they have important roles to play in deliberative situations (*Rhetoric* 2.1378a). He held that emotions such as pity, shame and friendship were connected to our capacity to judge issues and choose courses of action (*Rhetoric* 1378a22–24). The political emotions of anger, honour and their relatives help give citizens the mixture of 'sympathy and detachment' (*Rhetoric* 1368b–1369a) that makes for good practical judgement. His theory centres around the conception that emotions and reason are not separate components of the psyche but rather that neither can operate without the influence of the other (or can even be made to do so entirely [*Rhetoric* 1356a]). Following Aristotle, Nussbaum (1986: 214) supports the cooperation of reason and emotion and warns that

> if we starve and suppress emotions and appetites, it may be at the cost of so weakening the entire personality that it will be unable to act decisively; perhaps it will cease to act altogether.

This view conflicts with the approach taken by proponents of democratic deliberation who, by adopting critical argumentation as the only acceptable method of communication, treat citizens as if they were solely intellects, without emotions. This approach is not conducive to effective decision-making within deliberation, however, because, as Cicero noted, 'men decide far more problems by hate, love, lust, rage, sorrow, joy, hope, fear, illusion, or some other inward emotion than by reality, or authority or any legal standard, or judicial precedent, or statute' (*de*

Oratore 2.178). Emotions engage judgement rather than obscure it, and we believe (following Aristotle, Cicero and Young) that citizens' decision-making capacity is enhanced by the collaboration of reason and emotion, a position made impossible by the purely rational deliberation required by Plato, Habermas and Benhabib.

Furthermore, the judgements we make cannot be conceptualised as the outcome of a single motivational cause, but are rather the result of a wide and variable combination of competing motivations. That rhetoric requires an emotional connection between the speaker and the audience, often reveals these motivations and situated interests, and provides opportunities for the development of critical faculties. Citizens come to view each other not as passive consumers but as autonomous deliberators who are deserving of respect and whose practical judgement deserves to be engaged, not just through logical, reasoned argumentation but by speakers who stir up their emotions to execute particular emotional reactions from them. Exposure to persuasive and emotive appeals of this sort is a positive attribute of rhetoric within deliberation precisely because it necessitates that citizens engage their critical faculties and employ their powers of practical reasoning in the realisation that 'empathy, emotion and reason are all necessary ingredients' (Connolly 2007: 148) in making judgement and that deliberative decision-making should be informed not just by critical argumentation but by all aspects of personality and experience.

Aristotle repeats in *Nicomachean Ethics* (10.9) that the best deliberative judgements are made when individual emotional responses are subjected to criticism by the rational awareness of circumstances and events. This does not equate to emotion being dominated by reason but rather requires that the germane faculties work in tandem. That rhetorical communication affords importance to persuasive appeal to the emotions allows participants in democratic deliberation to develop critical skills in analysing 'the various ways something can be said, which colour and condition its substantive content' (Young 2002: 64–65), and this presents opportunities in the classroom for richer critical analysis. But what if speakers do not have the good of the community as their core purpose? The abuse of rhetoric for self-seeking ends will now be examined.

The challenge from self-interest

Having argued that appeal to the emotions is a positive attribute of rhetoric and useful when used in democratic deliberation, we now sound a note of caution by identifying that there are hazards involved with excessive appeals to emotion. If used inappropriately, rhetoric can be made to serve self-interest, and persuasion can work against the common good, both outcomes which are incompatible with the aim of democratic deliberation. By outlining Plato's concerns in this regard, we show that there are risks involved for commitment to reason and truth but, following Aristotle, that rhetoric itself is, indeed, compatible with the search for truth (and by extension the common good). Democratic education, we propose, ought to include some training in civic virtues, and we suggest that rhetoric can provide a useful forum for the acquisition, exercise and development of excellence in such virtues as thinking and speaking for noble purposes within deliberative democracy.

Plato expresses concern that rhetoric aims at the gratification of citizens and claims that by neglecting the common good and privileging self-interest, orators treat 'the people like children, attempting only to please them' (*Gorgias* 502d). In aiming to please the passions and appetites, rather than to instruct or improve the mind and soul, Plato treats rhetoric as a matter of obscurantism and denies that it is an art, claiming that it is but an imitation of an art, in that it does not rest upon a true knowledge of its object (*Gorgias* 453a). He points to the ability of orators to argue both sides of an issue as evidence for their lack of true knowledge. For Plato, reason leads to a single, simple truth. He concluded that the orators' ability to use clever words for diverse positions goes against reason and hinders the discovery of truth.

> He whose speaking is an art will make the same thing appear to the same persons at one time just and at another, if he wishes, unjust... he will make the same things seem to the State at one time good and at another the opposite.
> (*Phaedrus* 261d)

In such a way, then, Plato thought that orators used rhetoric to make 'the weaker account look the stronger' (Schiappa 1999: 54) in an effort to improve their own individual position within society, 'to save one's own skin to wrest a liberty which is only license, and to take power at any cost' (*Gorgias* 466c, 486a–d) (Pernot 2005: 47). Socrates even has the Sophists Polus and Callicles admit (*Gorgias* 466c, 486a–d) that political rhetoric is designed 'to pursue the competitive advantage of the orator, at the expense of his adversaries and auditors, by means of duplicitous, emotionally manipulative speeches'[6] (Shiffman 2004: 99). Such a disregard for truth is potentially problematic for contemporary theories of democratic deliberation which aim at the common good[7] and rely on commitments to inclusion, equality and reason from participants (Hicks 2002). What must be remembered here, though, is that Polus, Callicles and Gorgias were Sophists who were committed to the pursuit of power without regard to any ethical motive (*Gorgias* 452e), thus they do not represent the best use of rhetoric in society. Plato describes rhetoric as a producer of persuasion (*Gorgias* 453a) used by orators who behave like vultures, swooping on and attacking vulnerable prey (Garsten 2009: 177).[8] Within such a conception of rhetoric, the orator has no need to know the truth about that which he speaks, rather he simply has to discover a 'technique of persuasion so as to appear among the ignorant to have more knowledge than the expert' (*Gorgias* 459d). He, therefore, has no knowledge of what is right or wrong, noble or base, just or unjust; he is simply pleasing the people and pretending to be knowledgeable for the sake of securing his own ends.

Plato's concerns regarding rhetoric's potential to deceive are shared by Kant, who viewed rhetoric as 'the art of deluding by means of a fair semblance' (1951: 53). In the forum of civil law, he considered rhetoric unsuitable because it allowed for 'talking people over and of captivating them for the advantage of any chance person' (Kant 1951: 171). For Kant, as for Plato, it was through an appeal to the passions that the orators moved and deceived their audiences. He warned that rhetoric robbed 'their verdict of its freedom' (1951: 192) by winning over men's minds to the side of the speaker using coercive power to deny autonomous decision-making, thereby preventing adequate opportunity for reason to weigh the matter.

By concentrating on the abuse of rhetoric to serve the nefarious ends of sophists, politically ambitious, vain-glorious men, Plato is simply identifying one of many vices to be found in the public arena, and we consider that his dissatisfaction would be better directed towards the men, not the realm of rhetoric. Aristotle clarifies this point: nothing makes an argument, claim or position persuasive in the abstract (*Rhetoric* 1356b27). It has to convince another person, who, as we saw above in Aristotle's account of deliberative rhetoric, will have an individual character and will be subject to various irrational (as well as rational) influences. Persuasion in the strict sense identifies a way of influencing that is neither manipulation nor pandering. The speaker who manipulates his audience in order to bring them to a belief or action without their consent, as Kant thought orators moved men 'like machines' (1951: 5. 328n), has not persuaded but coerced. In contrast, the speaker who merely finds out where his audience itches and then scratches there, as Plato thought pandering Athenian orators did, has failed to change his listeners' minds at all. To truly persuade people is to induce them to change their own beliefs and desires in response to what has been said.

Although the passive voice is used, 'being persuaded', we recognise the difference between being persuaded and being indoctrinated or brainwashed; the difference lies in the active independence that is preserved when we are persuaded. An orator does not coerce; he merely puts words into the air. Therefore rhetoric does not bring about a mindless conformity in its adherents, moving people 'mass-like (Plato), crowd-like (Kierkegaard) and herd-like (Nietzsche)' (Jost and Hyde 1997: 10). This allegation ignores the part to be played by members of the audience. In the brief moments of conscious or unconscious reflection that occur while we listen to a sales pitch or a campaign speech, an active process of evaluation and assimilation occurs in our minds (Garsten 2009: 7), enabling us to make a judgement. The extent to which that judgement is influenced by the choice and arrangement of words depends on the extent to which the audience is willing to be persuaded.

Factors governing the willingness of the audience to be persuaded include the ethical education of the orator, the ethical education of the audience and the extent to which the audience has the opportunity to develop critical faculties when digesting communication within the public sphere. Admittedly, there is nothing inherent to the art of rhetoric which prevents its use for unethical ends.

Reciprocity within deliberation becomes untenable, and moral transparency is occluded when the commitment to the common good is sacrificed for reasons of self-interest. There are inescapable tensions here, between Aristotle's claim that rhetoric, used justly, can do much good (*Rhetoric* 1355b) and its infamy for being a powerful instrument of public thinking that can be used deceptively, to make a bad argument look good (Walton 2004: 297). However, rhetoric still offers something a democratic polity should desire: non-coercive persuasion, which is fundamental to the ethics of deliberative democracy (Chambers 1996). The solution lies not in removing rhetoric from deliberation but rather in educating against the abuse of rhetorical power through appropriate citizenship education. It is likely that this 'should be directed at least in part to the sorts of virtues that promote the ethical use of power' (Bentley 2004: 132) and should equip students with skills to distinguish the dispositions or states of character that tend to undermine the exercise of civic virtues. In this regard, rhetoric has a valuable role to play in helping citizens to recognise that ethical, evaluative and emotional climates determine the form and extent of persuasion.

The misuse of rhetoric and excessive appeal to emotions undoubtedly bring hazards. Yack (2006: 433) reminds us that 'emotions help us judge the value of competing proposals, [but] we must be willing to accept the risks that they will mislead us as well'. The best defence against the abuse of power is the wide distribution of power. Since rhetoric is a linguistic form of power and it can be taught, it follows that it *should* be taught. The power rhetoric provides has to be supported by a sound ethical grounding since the way rhetoric is practised will depend on the moral character of the practitioner. Since moral character is something that is developed through education, rhetorical practice will only ever be as good as the broader education citizens receive, so, following Aristotle (*Rhetoric* 2.6.1106a), we propose that ethical learning must be studied alongside the art of rhetoric. Cicero suggests that citizens, if they allow their reason and emotions to work in tandem as Aristotle suggested, need not be disengaged hearers of the sweet music of a speech (*de Oratore* 2. 33–34), pleased and gratified by speakers' rhetoric, but rather they can become trained listeners of music (*aures eruditae*), judging orators by their *logos*, *pathos* and *ethos* (Connolly 2007: 127). It is this training of critical faculties and orienting of moral compasses which should enable citizens to filter the positive uses of rhetoric from the corrupt ones. In democratic deliberation, citizens can think collectively and citizens (interpreted maximally as discussed in Chapter 2) should engage their critical faculties to consider the best course of action not just for themselves but for others.

Instead of isolating rhetoric from democratic deliberation because it can be misused to serve the self-interest of the few, a more fruitful approach views rhetoric as a communicative framework for the exchange of ideas, which permits the additional benefits of learning about the governance of reason and emotion. By exercising the critical faculties to develop filters for rhetoric's ethical and unethical use, then, citizens have the opportunity to develop critical skills at a deeper level than if communication within deliberation were restricted to critical argumentation. Crucial, though, is that individuals must have equal capacity to advance persuasive claims (Knight and Johnson 1997: 282). We have argued that rhetoric provides a structured, accessible and common framework for communication, which facilitates equal participation, but we now consider whether this notion of dialogue is fundamentally incompatible with classical rhetorical theory.

The challenge from monology

In addition to the challenges presented by rhetoric's emotional appeal and its potential abuse for self-interest, it is also criticised by contemporary democrats[9] because, as a monological form of communication used by a speaker to persuade an audience with no right of reply, it does not meet the moral requirement of equal political participation in deliberation. As outlined in Chapter 1, rhetoric originated from the need for Greeks to represent themselves through the articulation of their rights to settle disputes after tyranny was overthrown. In this sense, rhetoric was conceived as a monological endeavour which involved one man speaking for each 'side' of an issue, others listening, then voting to determine the outcome. Although Aristotle hints at a time in the fifth century BCE when deliberative rhetoric was used for the collective consideration of the best course of action for a community of citizens to take through reasoned (and impassioned) communication, since the formal structuring of the parts of speech developed by Cicero and Quintilian in the Roman era, rhetoric has once again become a pursuit associated with the delivery of speeches in agonistic civic circumstances.

Herein lies a problem: deliberation, nowadays, is meant to be a forum for the exchange of ideas (Chambers 2009), and contemporary theories of democratic deliberation[10] look to conversation as an ideal. Conversation is a dialogical method of speaking which, not relying on a defined structure, is at odds with the classical conception of rhetoric, which, being rooted in competition, manifested itself in carefully structured speeches delivered in conflictive environments like debates. The monological nature of rhetoric (the lack of provision for ongoing discussion) is difficult to reconcile with democratic deliberation as it is currently conceived. What follows is justification for a partly revised conception of rhetoric.

In order to maximise rhetoric's contribution in current conditions, certain characteristics of classical rhetorical theory must be abandoned. The monological nature of rhetoric, which demanded adherence to one's original persuasive appeal, must be relaxed in favour of an openness to 'learning from, and being challenged by' (Simpson 2001: 89) the views of other citizens. This can also include the dialogical element of adjusting their position to suit audience and circumstances. In a refinement of the adversarial nature of rhetoric, we suggest that in today's democracy, it could be more usefully oriented towards collaboration and compromise. This does not necessarily entail the abolishment of rhetoric to make room for conversation, however, since there could be potential risks with conversation. For Cicero, conversation (*sermo*) was a theoretical activity designed to uncover and explore philosophical questions conducted in private by elite and aristocratic men. That conversation is more suited to small groups than to an assembly is highlighted by Shiffman (2004: 110), who admits that it represents a 'formidable cognitive therapy, a reasonable method for improvement and is good for the soul' but is a peculiar way to get large groups of people with common and divergent interests to agree to bind themselves to a particular course of action. Conversation can only lead to further conversation, discussion to more discussion and in a deliberative sphere where issues of civic importance need to be debated and a consensus reached,[11] the structure provided by the rhetorical framework offers a possible benefit in this regard. In contrast to the private domain in which Cicero viewed conversation, he saw rhetoric as a method of communication more suited to a wider, open and popular forum. In such a context, it was a political and moral enterprise which aimed to persuade an audience or assembly to act in a particular way.

Rhetoric, as the art of persuasion, aims to culminate in a conclusive decision since the proponent of the argument already has an agenda; a viewpoint or thesis that he/she wants the others to accept, unlike deliberation, which is more open to alternative courses of action and is usually more collaborative in nature (Walton 2004: 310). We suggest that the classical conception of rhetoric ought to be revised, and its meaning reshaped, to accelerate consensus through multi-way oral exchange between participants. For this to be so, there must be more willingness than in the ancient model to develop and evolve one's position for the good of the community. This does not, however, have to be the result of an exclusive focus on common ground: in valorising only what we have in common, there is a missed opportunity to cultivate genuine 'respect for difference... commensurate with the justice requirement central to the deliberative model' (Healy 2011: 298). Rather, the tenability of each party's views needs to be held open to critical intersubjective appraisal in appropriately structured discursive forms (Healy 2011: 303), and it is here that rhetoric is essential in situating critical faculties at the centre of democratic deliberation. The eventual decision, far from being imposed by force or other nefarious means, issues out of the rhetorical and competitive struggle for advantage located within the public space of deliberation. In such a way, we assert, the persuasive and focussed style of rhetorical communication can contribute positively to democratic deliberation both by allowing the force of the best argument to win and by helping citizens foster the rhetorical skills of critical listening, constructing arguments and, most importantly within deliberation, engaging in argumentation.

The use of classical rhetoric, then, in contemporary conceptions of democratic deliberation has been shown to survive, relatively unscathed, three key challenges. Rhetoric can help support equality in deliberation through promoting the understanding of difference, because it necessarily involves seeing situations from the other's perspective. It is more suitable for democratic deliberation, in this regard, than storytelling or greeting, since it offers greater accessibility to meaning through a single communicative framework designed for use in the public sphere. Furthermore, the presentation of both sides of the issue and the prior consideration given to the views of others within the rhetorical framework may expedite the decision-making process more than storytelling and greeting, which are likely to facilitate ongoing discussion but may not be conducive to decision-making or collective action, owing to their lack of focussed argumentation. Both in streamlining the deliberation process and in moving beyond communication focussed on logic to include identification with opposing views, rhetoric represents an improvement on argumentation within democratic deliberation.

By appealing to the emotions, rhetoric admits input from non-rational aspects of the psyche, which, according to Aristotle, makes for better civic deliberation than purely reason-based methods of communication. While rhetoric need not aim at the common good and can be abused for self-interest, Aristotle says that the abuse of rhetoric is no worse than the abuse of other things (*Rhetoric* 1.1.1355b). Since nothing is persuasive in itself, the use of rhetoric within deliberation represents an opportunity for citizens within democracy to cultivate critical reason and ethical conduct by reflecting on, and evaluating, communication which appeals to their reason, passions, appetites and emotions – material which is more richly critical than rational argumentation alone.

The most challenging objection to rhetoric undoubtedly stems from the tension between argumentation and conversation: unfortunately, being monological from its inception, rhetoric is not easily reconcilable with conversation or discussion. Rhetoric may help to present a persuasive pitch or accelerate consensus within deliberation by arguing opposing sides of an issue, but we acknowledge that its agonistic approach is of value only in public and formal settings for deliberation. Rhetoric as a method of persuasive communication has limited relevance to more informal deliberative settings, which rely on ongoing exchange through conversation and which are considered vital stages[12] within the democratic deliberative process (Hauser 2008), so a partly revised conception of rhetoric is needed.

We propose that the strict divisions of the parts of speech of the rhetorical framework are relaxed, rhetorical communication is used for multi-logic purposes, and there is a heightened commitment from all participants to the capacity of rhetoric to move all parties to new ground rather than narrowly to 'win' one's case. A healthy deliberative democracy requires the exercise of the critical faculties, and we have explained ways in which rhetoric can contribute positively to the cultivation of critical skills: through critical argumentation, *ethopoeia* and *refutatio*. Yet if rhetoric is to enjoy a revival in public deliberation, it must eschew narrow historical and political agendas and 'reemphasise the practical tools of democratic citizenship' (Hogan 2008: 82), which we have identified as communicating responsibly by listening and speaking for noble purposes and exercising critical skills informed by robust ethical standards. This mirrors very closely Aristotle's suggestion regarding deliberative rhetoric from 2500 years ago; and in suggesting that a useful way to improve civic engagement is by looking to 'some of the oldest traditions in rhetorical theory and practice' rather than new information technologies, Hogan (2008: 77), we think, is right.

To bring this theoretical chapter to a close, we present a case study.

CASE STUDY: Matt Pinkett

When I took over as head of English at a school where aspirations were low, I was struck not just by the dismal pass rates but by the sheer lack of belief in what students thought they could achieve. Walking into the classroom, I remember seeing the prescribed persuasive writing curriculum: teach the children the AFOREST acronym,[1a] then ask them to produce some uninspired letter about banning school uniforms or persuading the canteen to serve pizza every Friday. It was mechanical and lifeless, and it left me deflated. Something had to change.

I had recently immersed myself in books on Aristotelian rhetoric, and the possibilities they opened up were electrifying. *Ethos*, *pathos*, *logos* – the very foundations of persuasive communication – were not abstract concepts; they were tools these students could wield. Beyond that, I discovered rhetorical figures with names that sounded like spells: *polysyndeton*, *hypophora*, *epistrophe*, *syllogism*. I learned how arguments could be structured with the classical *exordium*, *narratio*, *divisio*, *proof*, *refutation* and *peroration*. For the first time, I saw persuasive writing as art rather than a checkbox exercise.

We started by teaching the children about Aristotle himself, not as a distant historical figure but as a thinker who could illuminate the way they understood and expressed ideas. We encouraged them to think critically about rhetoric: how arguments could persuade, how words could shape belief and how to challenge assumptions with elegance and logic. Before, the students had only paintbrushes; now, with classical rhetorical theory, we gave them the paint. Suddenly, their writing had texture, depth and colour.

Alongside rhetoric, we introduced Greek stories to Year 7 students. The *Iliad* became our first text, a gateway into a world of epic narrative, moral complexity and human drama. The transformation was immediate. Children who had previously slumped in their seats were captivated. They argued over Achilles' choices, empathised with Hector, and began to see the power of storytelling as a means of exploring the human condition. Their curiosity grew, as did their confidence in thinking and writing. What had once been a rote exercise was now a living dialogue between ancient wisdom and contemporary voices.

The impact of this approach went beyond exam results. Students began to understand that their ideas mattered, that their words could influence, persuade and move others. They saw themselves not just as passive recipients of knowledge but as creators, thinkers and storytellers. Introducing Classics into a mainstream curriculum was not about elitism; it was about empowerment (Hazell, 2020). It provided a framework for critical thinking, for imaginative engagement and for cultivating a sense of intellectual ambition. In giving them Aristotle and Homer, we gave them the tools to imagine what they could become – and, in the process, we began to rewrite the story of the school itself.

Notes

1 The other two are forensic (law court speeches) and epideictic (eulogies).

1a AFOREST stands for Alliteration, Facts, Opinion, Rhetorical question, Emotive language, Statistics, Three (rule of).

2 This connection is informed 'by historic–mythical narratives, as well as by more personal memories of life in the community' (Bentley 2004: 130), which play an important part in forming identity and discourse within democratic dialogue. There is a schism, then, between those who consider that deliberation takes place between people who are basically the same (for whom the restriction of speaking style to critical argumentation limits the negative impact of difference) and those who acknowledge that citizens are not uniformly positioned (for whom self-expression is considered to be a matter of personal preference).

3 The extent to which consensus ought to be regarded as the end of deliberation is contested (Bohman 1996, Young 1997, Chambers 2003, 2009, Dryzek 2010). Clearly, citizens need to make decisions, but if consensus is required, it is likely that the most dominant participants in deliberation will 'win'. This endangers the inclusive nature of the process.

4 This is Nussbaum's term and encompasses a broad meaning including 'cultivating powers of imagination that are essential to citizenship... [and] the capacity for sympathetic imagination which will enable us to comprehend the motives and choices of people different from ourselves, seeing them not as forbiddingly alien and other, but as sharing many problems and possibilities with us' (Nussbaum 1997: 85).

5 As was explained earlier in this chapter, Benhabib comments that rhetoric 'moves people and achieves results without having to render an account of the bases upon which it induces people to engage in certain courses of action rather than others' (Benhabib 1996: 83).

6 The abuse of rhetoric was not limited to the Sophists in classical Athens. Cicero tells how orators sometimes used ethically objectionable techniques which philosophers would find 'not only wanting in discretion but positively unseemly and disgraceful' (*de Oratore* 1.53.227). The space of politics in ancient Rome, more than in Greek democracy, was filled by dispute, contingency, inconsistency, unreason and passion, hence why Roman politics were awash with orators who sought to distort the public good by fooling citizens into allowing the interest of some partial association to claim their loyalties rather than thinking of the good of the whole. This individualistic or 'interest-based' model (Healy 2011: 297) was, at times, used as a technique of deception: 'Cicero had boasted that he had thrown dust in the eyes of the jury in the case of Cluentius' (Quintilian, *Instituto Oratoria* 2.17.21).

7 At this stage, it is important to acknowledge that a considerable number of tensions surround the extent to which democratic deliberative theory aims at justice and/or truth and the extent to which it relies on shared moral commitments and/or reason (Benhabib 1996, Knight and Johnson 1997, Hauser and Benoit-Barne 2002, Hicks 2002, Young 2002, Chambers 2003, 2009). We do not propose to address these issues in detail since they are not of primary importance to this book. Instead, we restrict our discussion to an exploration of ways in which the potential abuse of rhetoric for the purpose of self-interest can be reconciled with its use as the most desirable method of communication within democratic deliberation.

8 Plato depicts the citizenry (*demos*) as one that was 'easy to manipulate, gullible, distracted and lacking motivation for the task of self-governance' (McDorman and Timmerman 2008: xv), so Garsten's simile here is apt in representing the Sophists as predatory.

9 Benhabib's (2002) commitment to 'egalitarian reciprocity' maintains that each individual has the same symmetrical rights to various speech acts, to initiate new topics and to ask for reflection about the presuppositions of the conversation. Equality also dominates Bohman's (1996: 16) list of the basic normative requirements and constraints on deliberation.

10 Walzer (1990), Bohman (1996), Remer (1999, 2000).

11 As was highlighted earlier, this is a contested area of deliberative theory (see Manin 1987, Bohman 1998 and Dryzek 2010 for more extended treatment of the tensions) which cannot be fully investigated here.

12 Deliberation ought to be about the quality of the thinking, speaking and listening, so the number of citizens involved is not important. Chambers (2009) suggests that informal conversation between citizens is as deliberative as the delivery of critical argumentation in mass democracy.

PART B
Cultivating rhetoric and critical literacy in schools

4 The purpose and construct of rhetoric and critical literacy in schools

The purpose of rhetoric

At this point, it would be helpful for us to take the considerations and provocations presented so far and turn them into a tangible set of principles for what comes next. If we are to set ambitions for every child to be taught rhetoric as part of their educational experience in this country, then we are required to consider the subject knowledge of rhetoric as a domain in and of itself, what it sets out to achieve and how we bring this to life in the classroom.

For the context of educational experience, rhetoric enables learners to become judges of communication, to read nuance and manipulation, and in turn, master navigation of this as a consumer, critically engaging with language and finally, mastering the art of doing this themselves through taught examples. Schools will wish to consider this vision and intention in keeping with their own philosophy of curriculum and ensure that their vision statement to stakeholders makes explicit this intention as part of their overall provision. If the schools' vision is 'to provide a curriculum that moves beyond the academic needs of students, providing rich and memorable experiences that ensures all students are confident communicators of the future', then we must consider rhetoric as the knowledge base through which students will develop such a confidence. After all, you cannot be a confident communicator unless you know how to communicate well, across a range of contexts with a number of requirements and parameters of play and have seen multiple examples of this employed effectively to develop a sense of mastery for yourself.

- Schools should consider rhetoric as a vehicle through which students will write, read and communicate effectively within taught content and the wider world around them
- School leaders should therefore stress test to what degree their current intention and ambition for the curriculum claims to fulfil this component of student learning and experience and adapt accordingly

DOI: 10.4324/9781003409069-6

How rhetoric manifests as a domain of knowledge, skill and understanding

Before we delve into the exciting task of curating rhetoric as a taught domain, it is worth exploring what we aim to achieve as a result of the intention laid out in Part A. If a student acquires sufficient knowledge to be classified as an expert in rhetoric, relative to their educational journey but with firm foundations for next steps of study if they choose to do so, what might that look like? Perhaps a distillment of this would be:

- To be critical of others' communication (written and spoken)
- To adopt a critical approach to one's own communication (written and spoken)

To be able to critically think on the quality of written and spoken manipulation of language, it is therefore pivotal to have a deep understanding of the technicalities and artistry of language itself.

A note on critical thinking

Teaching rhetoric helps to teach critical thinking.[1] Indeed, Willingham (2019) outlines,

> In free societies, the ability to think critically is viewed as a cornerstone of individual civic engagement and economic success. We may disagree about which content students should learn, but we at least agree that, whatever they end up learning, students ought to think critically about it.[2]

Critical thinking has been variously described as 'the correct assessment of statements' (Ennis 1962: 83), 'reasonable, reflective thinking that is focussed on deciding what to believe or to do' (Ennis 1981: 143) and

> [a] student's ability to be accurate and seek accuracy, be clear and seek clarity, be open-minded, restrain impulsivity, take a position when the situation warrants it, and be sensitive to the feelings and level of knowledge of others.
>
> (Marzano, Pickering and McTighe [1993] in Bers 2005: 16)

The ability to decide what to believe, in a wide variety of contexts, is, in our view, an especially important tool to have in modern life. The etymological root of 'critical' is '*kritikos*' in classical Greek which means 'judge' so thinking critically must, by necessity, aim to make some sort of judgement. School leaders, teachers and students require training in methods of assessing, analysing and decoding information, which allows them to critically examine their own stance and arrive at a considered judgement which they are subsequently able to justify.

How, then, can we teach critical thinking? This is worthy of exploration, because by teaching students how language is constructed to evoke meaning and to nudge a specific interpretation, we are moving them from comprehension to critical thinking.

The notion of critical thinking is taken from principles of transfer: we firstly teach students the principles and protocols of a sequence within a subject, they practices this with expert guidance removed over time so that, once mastered, they will transfer the approach to a new context and use it to make sensible decisions, judgements or evaluations. For instance, if we were taught how to complete an oil change, we would need expert input to:

- Know how to determine when an oil change is required
- See the process modelled and apply this to practising multiple times myself
- Be taught the common pitfalls and how to anticipate and avoid them
- Apply this to a range of different vehicles and know the pitfalls and considerations for specific models

The knowledge building and exemplification must take place before we are able to think critically and independently in this specific area through transferring what we know to an entirely new context.[3] For rhetoric, the same principles apply, and so in this chapter, we will consider the knowledge base of rhetoric as a domain and what must be applied, practised and mastered to enable students to then think critically about the construction and curation of written and spoken words. It helps to ensure that we think of critical thought within the domain itself, as opposed to critical thought as a sub-domain that exists in isolation and is therefore taught in a vacuum.

For leaders and teachers, in the same way that we leverage the national curriculum for phase and subject,we should:

- Consider the identity of an expert student – what they know, are able to do and what they understand
- Consider the journey of progression through the big ideas or key concepts of rhetoric
- Consider the foundational knowledge that students require of the domain to ensure meaningful critical engagement at a later point
- The opportunities available to students to apply and practise this knowledge

The construct of rhetoric

For the purposes of primary or secondary education, we will primarily focus on deliberative rhetoric: the act of persuasion and how language is structured or shaped to manipulate, influence or move a group of people to a specific course of action. In this section, we will make a proposal for such a framework, with the understanding that other theories and models for rhetoric exist (though predominantly for the purposes of adult education) and that this is simply a suggestion to shape school leaders' and teachers' thinking.

Rhetoric (including critical hermeneutics, metalanguage, critical reading and discourse analysis) provides a tool-kit, we suggest, which helps learners develop literacy, critical thinking and critical literacy skills. It gives them a valuable and relevant method for seeing beyond the veil of verbiage, the occluding 'rhetoric' surrounding every aspect of daily life from schooling to politics and advertising.

These skills correlate closely with the *inventio* (planning stage), the *disposito* (arrangement) and the *refutatio* (refutation of the opponent's argument) stages of the rhetorical framework. These steps all involve the ability to select and organise information, offering opportunities for the exercise and improvement of both critical thinking skills and literacy skills. There has been much criticism (Knight 1992, Brown 1998, Barnes 2005, Paul 2005) of educational trends which fail to teach students the fundamentals of argumentation with the result that students are unable to break arguments down into premises and conclusions, and to spot common fallacies, leaving them oblivious to 'questionable classifications, unknowable or questionable statistics and covert biases' (Knight 1992: 66).

There are already alternative pedagogical methods which seek to address these deficiencies in the teaching of argumentation. For example, Beyer (1988) recommends for text production the formulation and execution of basic step-by-step approaches for problem solving: recognition, representation, formulation of a solution plan, execution and evaluation. Browne and Keeley (1986) and Knight (1992: 67) teach frameworks of interpretation which require students to (a) identify the presence of an argument, (b) delineate conclusions and premises, including missing premises, (c) analyse each premise independently, including any common fallacies associated with the premise, (d) ask what other information or points of view should be considered and (e) determine, finally, if they are persuaded to accept the conclusion and for what reasons. Our provocation is this: why not just teach rhetoric?

Knowledge of the whole rhetorical framework (covered in Chapter One) requires that orators think critically about the evaluation of components, including definition, cause, consequence and effect, both when constructing and analysing communication. Current pedagogical approaches are limited to either construction or analysis; this effectively doubles the learning required by students and does not offer as efficient an approach as the combined approach encapsulated by rhetoric for the study of argumentation. Secondly, the inclusion of the *refutatio* in the rhetorical framework requires deeper critical thinking skills because it compels students to put themselves in another person's situation (usually their opponent) and forces them to see the world as 'the other' sees it, requiring them to frame questions that they might otherwise never ask (Knight 1992: 68). The *refutatio* requires students of rhetoric to go beyond the basic critical thinking needed to consider possible approaches and construct one position, to actually articulate an incisive counter-argument and provide justification for their own stronger position. In this way, the rhetorical framework model not only delivers the opportunity for critical thinking skills but actually demands a higher-order skill from students, one they will undoubtedly find challenging, but which promises to enhance their cognitive understanding and reasoning abilities.

Once the key ideas and the structure of the argument have been identified and organised, consideration must be given to how best to communicate these to the audience, which requires the application of critical literacy skills.

Critical literacy

Like critical thinking, critical literacy requires the exercise of judgement but in relation to the construction and deconstruction of communication. In this sense, it combines elements of critical thinking and literacy. At its simplest level, it appears to be concerned with the ability to state the main purpose of a text and draw inferences. At its more complex level, it is a method of approaching discourse that foregrounds and questions power relations[4] (Shor and Pari 1999: 21). At its most complex, it acts as an impetus towards change, encouraging learners to take on the world at large and, by understanding systems of injustice, to arm themselves to challenge those systems of privilege and power (Cooper and White 2006: 31). It calls for a predisposition to deconstruct and critique all forms of discourse, exposing systems of dominance, oppression and advantage (Cooper and White 2006, Stevens and Bean 2007).

Macro level: a lens through which students can understand and critically engage with rhetoric

Appeals: what are *ethos*, *logos* and *pathos*?

Aristotle proposed that an orator was successful when he communicated with an audience through three key appeals:

Logos: appealing to reason. *Logos* can be thought of as the logic, reason and substantive nature of the argument. This is perhaps demonstrated through expert input, the use of well-selected evidence to support a position within an argument, or the extent to which the writer has argued their point. It is the substance for argument itself as a method of manipulation: for instance, that a doctor might be used within an opinion piece to claim that heat therapy is proven to be effective to reduce inflammation, or when damning statistics from a recent study into illiteracy are used to argue about the quality of education in a particular country. *Logos* provides a sense of logic to the argument that gives the speaker or writer a position of authority to layer other methods of appeal.

Ethos: appealing to the writer or speaker's character, which then enables the audience to consider to what degree they hold credibility in the domain of their argument. Where *logos* appeals through reason, *ethos* appeals through credibility and character of the orator: why is this topic important to them? Do they speak or write from a place of vested interest? Are they qualified and pragmatic for this topic, and how do they demonstrate this? For example, a founder of an environmental charity may be speaking at an event on the eradication of poor practice around recycling, or a mother may write about the dangers of of poorly maintained public park equipment. The speaker will appear knowledgeable and trustworthy if they can 'walk the talk'.

Pathos: appealing to the emotions of the audience, which then moves a piece of writing or a speech from a declaration to a call to action or a moment of realisation. In the way that a volta will shift a poem, the employment of *pathos* will shift an argument through an invitation to the audience to respond emotionally to the topic of the argument. This may be an article outlining child poverty through the storytelling anecdote of an agonised parent and direct speech of the child; it may be the urgency of language to close a speech that pleads with the audience to take immediate action to prevent further lapses in criminal law regarding animal cruelty. Depictions may be vivid and deliberately constructed to provoke a reader's imagination as a way to achieve this. *Pathos* considers the role of the audience or reader in the argument and how they are moved to respond in a particular way.

Rhetorical triangle

This model (Figure 4.1), as a framework, makes multiple assumptions: that a skilled writer or speaker will strive to create a sense of balance across the three appeals, and that the curation of a text will draw from this model to make clear the purpose of the text and the intended response they hope to evoke in the audience.

- Leaders and teachers should consider this framework as a concept of quality for rhetoric

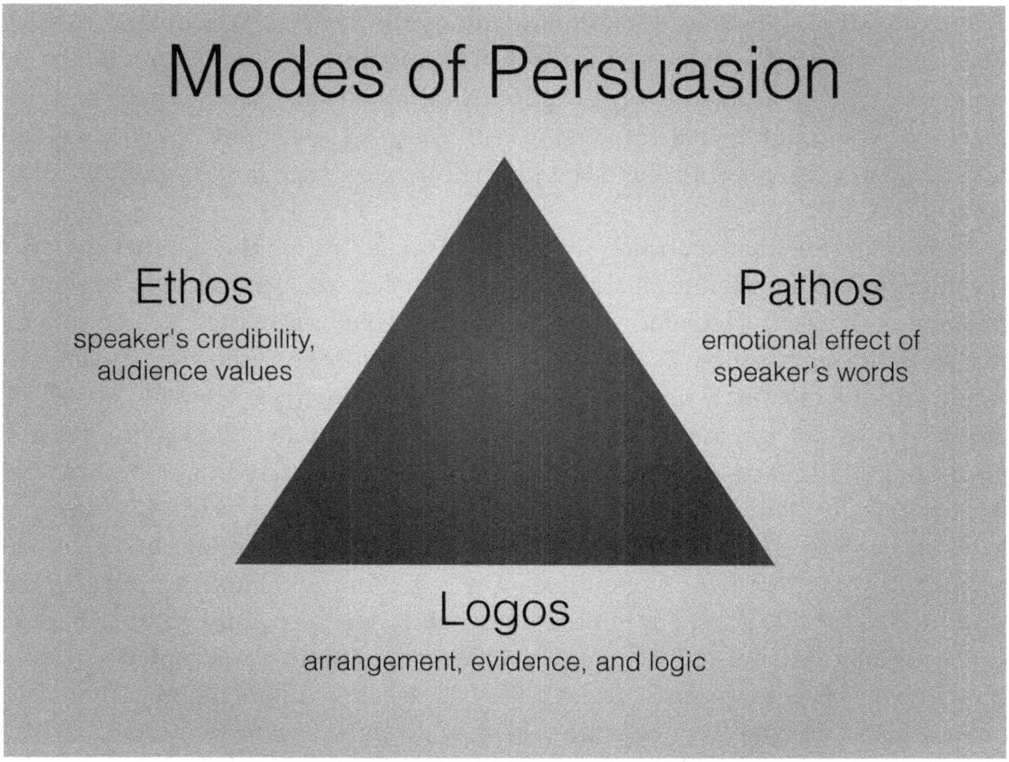

Figure 4.1 The Rhetorical Triangle

- The three appeals help to inform the selection of high-quality texts and speech exemplars for students to access
- Leaders and teachers should consider complexity and text construction that remains age-and stage-appropriate

It is also important to note that this framework should not be applied as isolated components that assemble a piece of writing, much as one might build a house: it is not one brick of the framework and then another. The appeals can be blurred so that sentences employ more than one aspect at the same time. For instance, 'I speak from experience' will appeal both to *ethos* – the credibility piece – as well as reason – the audience would attend to someone with substantive experiences in the field that they speak. There are also specific works that are deliberately emotive, but can be leveraged within a text to also position logic or reason. For example, Powell's reference to Dupoint in his infamously controversial 'Rivers of Blood' speech: 'Those whom the gods wish to destroy, they first make mad' (Powell 1968), taken from Reverend William Anderson Scott (1854) and repurposed in such a way to make the abhorrent seem scholarly.

The application of such a quotation positions the speaker as scholarly, whilst the emotive use of 'mad', given the topic of immigrants, as 'other', appeals to the sympathy of the audience, with a polite refusal of pity. Each appeal may be represented through layers of meaning within the text, with the knowledge that historical and social context and the place of the audience hold important roles here.

The use of this framework should not restrict schools to thinking that rhetoric is reduced to non-fiction texts and national speeches: once students have such a framework to use as a lens for reading or being the audience, they will be able to recognise the application of such appeals in a multitude of methods. For instance, Adele appeals to *ethos* when accepting the Sherry Lansing Leadership award ('I accept this leadership award as an invitation to carry on being myself.... It's got me quite far') to Maya Angelou's poem, Still I Rise! ('I rise up from a past rooted in pain'); from Johnnie Cochran's closing defence argument in the OJ Simpson trial that centred on *pathos* shaped by *logos* to the jury ('If it doesn't fit, you must acquit') to Greta Thunberg's employment of logos in her damning chastisement to world leaders ('Cutting our emissions in half in ten years only gives us a 50% chance of staying below 1.5 degrees... a 50% risk is simply not acceptable to us'). This framework dances across pages wherever we encounter a moment that captures the human condition, spanning subject disciplines and forms, in a bid to create memorable words that will nudge audience emotion or behaviours.

At a macro level, there is a broad analysis for teachers to consider and present as lines of enquiry when modelling to students the use of rhetoric as a framework for analysis before evaluation is possible.

- What is the nature of the speech or text – what are its ambitions or aims? How can we build up a comprehensive picture of this when considering time, place, person and social or historical climate? Who might it therefore advocate for, or oppose, in its making?
- Does it appeal to reason, emotion or character in its creation, and how do we get a sense of this? Where might there be a sense of balance or otherwise that supports us to form such an opinion?
- Can we ascertain its success through this macro-analysis? What images or calls to action are impressed upon the audience or reader, and would this be sufficient in moving them to action?

The value of high-quality texts

Before we discuss the application of specific rhetorical techniques within such texts, for subject leaders and teachers should consider how text choices are made to ensure that the text fulfils curriculum aims for both the subject and the study of rhetoric itself. Leaders and teachers may use the following principles.

Ensuring texts can be accessed by children depending on language, construction, context and maturity of topic

There are several incredible texts out there that will serve the exemplification of rhetoric well and yet be inaccessible to students as a result of their content, language, construction or even the particular themes explored within the texts. There can sometimes be a misconception that the prospect of challenge and ambition for the curriculum knows no ceiling, however, there are assurances to be sought when selecting the study of rhetoric as a valuable use of curriculum time. It would be advisable to consider the alignment between text complexity and whether children of the age and stage will be able to engage with the content or topics explored. There is merit in balancing ambition with accessibility.

A collection of diverse texts that illustrate a range of forms

All teachers are teachers of reading, and ensuring a breadth of texts enables children to appreciate so many different styles of writing, but also exposes them to a diversity of voices presented in texts. This is especially pertinent when teaching rhetoric, as we are giving children the opportunity to see how language is both framed and manipulated to feed a greater purpose: we choose whether to present heroes or villains of history in our text selection, or both. Through choices made regarding texts, we form pupils' models for polemic poetry; timeless political or social movement speeches; and advertisements that are remembered some twenty to thirty years later, as a result of the sophisticated use of rhetoric deeply ingrained in their curation. The reading spine of either an explicit unit of study for rhetoric, or the wider curriculum choices if considering engagement of rhetoric as a thread throughout the taught subject disciplines, will shape the understanding that pupils have of form and genre, as well as rhetorical awareness.

This stretches to the representation of diversity in our text choices: the authentic lived experiences of those figures who may not be immediately prolific in our canon or origin stories. Such choices ensure that children can see themselves reflected in the content they read, or alternatively, explore perspectives beyond their own.

Taking a stance on risk with reading

Studying rhetoric provides us with the opportunity – as with much of text selection and the curriculum – to open pupils' eyes to a wider world beyond their own understanding or experiences, which, after all, is the beauty of literature. It can sometimes be tempting to lean into the portrayal of safe topics, or the stereotypical presentation of characters: the male hero, perhaps; the war speech ahead of winning; the polemic speech that determined a successful outcome in history;

princesses as mute and Kings as eloquent. Texts exist not just to show the origin of such ideas, or avoidance of others, but the subversion of such ideas and the increasing emergence of others. These deliberate selections will move us closer to an examination not just for rhetorical exposure, but of the human condition itself.

Rhythm, pattern and familiarity

For the purpose of curriculum content, and especially where knowledge of the domain explored may be less familiar, as is the case for rhetoric study, finding texts that introduce children to the rhythms and patterns of language is hugely beneficial. When exploring rhetoric, it is often through a structural study that we recognise the way in which the audience or reader is being directed towards a particular path of thinking or behaviour, which is then further enhanced by word choice.

Moreover, we live in a world where the notion of re-reading a book must be well justified – it had better change your life to warrant casting your eyes over the pages of a book for the second time! We underestimate the power of revisiting texts through our taught curriculum. Learners might see the content through a new lens or they may make a comparison between a previously read text and the text currently under scrutiny. When knowledge could potentially be fragile, selecting texts to look back on as knowledge is acquired and applied in practice can be incredibly helpful in developing models for excellent creation by pupils.

Micro level: the arrangement of language

The initial macro-level of analysis, then, provides teachers with the opportunity to consider how they intend to teach a key set of rhetorical devices. As with teaching specific terms or techniques within a subject, it is helpful for us to move away from specific acronyms or shortcuts in a bid to make less familiar terms part of everyday language. Whilst a mnemonic might initially appear to support the student in memorising specific term names, in our experience, such an approach hinders mastery at a later point. This is because students will remember the term but not remember the intentionality with which to employ the term: in short, they remember the what, but not the why or how.

These techniques continue to be used in contemporary communication (Leith's [2011] book identifies numerous examples from the speeches of modern politicians), so the greater students' familiarity with their formation and possible manipulative effect, the more likely that they can decipher what is meant from the manner in which it is delivered. Surely the more informed students feel about language, the more confident they will be in applying their critical skills to the germane tasks[5] of construction and deconstruction?

The study of rhetoric at school equips students with the ability to recognise the use (and abuse) of these techniques in the communications they encounter through enhanced critical literacy skills, but rhetoric also improves their literacy skills by integrating these rhetorical techniques[6] into their own written and spoken communications. Rhetoric has a unique role to play in the curriculum by uniting these three cross-curricular skills into a single framework. In this way, it offers a more efficient pedagogical approach to curricular skills, which are currently treated separately and delivered in isolated ways by practitioners.

Here are some key terms that are commonplace in texts and speeches with which students should be familiar. We use the three appeals as a lens to embark upon this exploration. Note, often specific terms, when well employed, will have multi-layered purpose within a text, which we will consider shortly. Additionally, we have tried to detail where terms might be used to create a specific effect, though their employment is not limited to simply creating that one effect in isolation. Finally, whilst we have suggested a framework of devices as a starting point, we know that language is not this simplistic. More confident writers and readers will see the multi-purpose applications of these devices. In turn, they will develop develop their own models for how to use a plural pronoun to close in moving a reader to a thought or action, just as they might present a counter argument to open their appeal to *ethos*.

Rhetoric devices: core knowledge and framing for teaching

Cultivating a sense of *ethos*

Anecdote: often used to create a sense of credibility, a short, interesting story about a real incident or person. 'I can tell you the exact day that I realised I wasn't perfect'.

Hypophora: a question followed by a response. 'Do you think that stopped me? Of course not'.

Repetition: the emphasis created by repeating a word. Another embellishment of this is **Anaphora**: a word repeated at the beginning of successive clauses. A further adaptation for emphasis is a **tricolon**: a list of three within a sentence used for emphasis. 'I came, I saw, I conquered'.

Plural pronoun: use of we, our or us for a sense of collegiality. 'We know all too well what the future looks like'.

Appealing to *logos*

Proof: evidence to support ideas or opinions. This may be statistics, an expert opinion, facts or sound reasoning that supports the claim.

Dialysis: a sentence that poses two conflicting arguments. 'We can wage war or demand peace. We cannot do both'.

Hyperbole: exaggeration to emphasise a point or idea. 'Millions of us need this movement on policy'.

Imperative: a commanding statement that demands action. 'Forget any previous ideas'.

Appealing to *pathos*

Emotive language: word or phrase choice that intends to move the audience or reader to feel and therefore act. 'Smoking rips lives apart'.

Direct address: Use of a first person verb to elicit a response or behaviour from the audience. 'I need you to address this before it's too late'.

There are ten core terms here, which, if understood, practised and mastered, will enable pupils to become masters of persuasion in writing and reading. We may wish to introduce more complex terms at times in our curriculum provision (see Webster 2023 for student activities), but time and experience (and a lot of Kat banging her head against a table when teaching year eleven) have taught us that to teach core terms well with a confident sense of mastery will always yield better results than teaching a large number superficially.

Finally, it is worth remembering that these are simply terms. The created purpose(s) of the speaker and interpretation of reader should sit central to the process of analysis and critical evaluation. In the same way that we would handle historical source analysis, scientific hypothesis or literary analysis of character or theme, devices are simply giving names to the objects that enable the meaning and experience of the reader (or audience) for whom it is intended.

- Select high-quality exemplification that shows the rule, concept of quality and flexibility of rhetoric in action.
- Use both appeals and devices to draw out the interplay between writer/reader and orator/audience.

Rhetorical study as a map of progression

We have consequently established that the substance of a rhetoric curriculum is therefore:

- taught appeals
- a core set of rhetorical devices; and

- the careful selection of high-quality texts that exemplify both appeals and devices as a framework for manipulation or influence

In Chapter 5, we will explore the fundamental principles of curriculum design, but there is value in considering what a progression model looks like for teaching rhetoric. Especially when teaching content that may be unfamiliar to students, plotting the way that knowledge will be acquired and assimilated over time will then inform the design of curriculum materials. For instance, a team may plot out the initial engagement with, and revisiting of, content as follows:

Year 6

At this stage, students begin to notice persuasion in the world around them: in adverts, campaign posters, speeches and stories. The focus is on *recognition:* learning that language choices are deliberate and that words are used in an attempt to shape thought and behaviour.

Year 7

Students now move from recognising rhetorical meaning to comparing the strength of this across multiple texts. They learn how appeals work in combination, and how credibility, reason and emotion weave together to create a sense of balanced argument within written or spoken texts. An awareness of text choices being explored in History or Religious Education would be beneficial here.

Year 8

Students now revisit prior knowledge to develop an understanding of rhetoric in poetic form, considering the role that rhetoric can play within this form to respond to historical or societal debate. The contextual aspect of texts is made more explicit, and students may spend time using comparative study to build mental models for polemic poetry before attempting their own (highly dependent on the wider English curriculum sequence and prior knowledge of poetic form).

Year 9

Students build on knowledge acquired previously to consider the role that rhetoric plays in mainstream media or nuanced political debate. They can identify the use of rhetorical subversion and consider the effectiveness of a text or speech in this context, evaluating its capability to persuade the intended and unintended audiences. Content can be used to open a discussion about the ethics of rhetoric and the moral implications of using language to shape or influence behaviours.

Progression summary					
Stage	Conceptual focus	Text choices for exemplification	Rhetorical knowledge	Application of knowledge might be through	Teacher focus
Year 6	Recognition	Three forms (advertising, campaign posters, speech)	Appeals and structural arrangement of these; evoking of emotion through a text; four core devices	Identification of appeals and using this structure in written or spoken work; reading analysis of structure using model texts	Model identification of structural choices through the lens of appeals
Year 7	Application	Revisit three forms and use comparative study; use of articles	Interaction of appeals and meaning of four core devices/ revisiting previous core devices	Balance of appeals and using this in written or spoken work, including opinion pieces	Model purpose and balance argument
Year 8	Refining	Revisit forms and use comparative study; introduce polemic poetry	Audience manipulation through tone, register and context	Layering of appeals in reading and using this in written or spoken work, including polemic poetry	Model use of different tones and the impact of these
Year 9	Critical engagement	Revisit forms and use comparative study; introduce political debate	Rhetoric subversion; ethics of persuasion; evaluating the effectiveness of argument	Evaluate the effectiveness of rhetoric across extended argumentative pieces or engage in formal debate	Model evaluative judgement

This is for illustrative purposes and there would certainly be adaptations or variations informed by the wider curriculum provision; text forms and genres that students had already been exposed to; the sequence in which subjects of the arts are taught. There are several ways that a rhetoric course of study could further embellish an existing curriculum, or even the choice that teachers and leaders may make to teach as an explicit unit (and the strengths or limitations of doing so). Certainly, subject specialists and phase leads in primary will want to consider the 'epistemic ascent'[7] for students as they move towards the position of critical reasoning. As an English specialist, Kat found great success in leveraging earlier rhetoric study in Key Stage 3 when teaching Year 11 students unseen papers, or teaching Year 12 the role of gender within linguistic analysis. Similarly, students look at extreme speech, unvalidated opinion or fake news and conspiracy theories through an entirely different lens when they have the capability to inspect it under the rhetoric microscope, as it were.

Reading, speaking and writing when teaching rhetoric

When considering the construct of rhetoric for the purposes of teaching content, it is worth pausing over the three pillars through which subjects, especially the arts, will draw out application and practice, as well as text choices to act as model texts. Again, balance is key: to be able to write, students must be exposed to carefully selected model texts, but these texts must be used with intention by teachers, and grappled over by students. We have already specified the principles for choosing texts, and these texts will ultimately shape how students define rhetoric for themselves. It is therefore paramount that we honour the form of texts and capture them through teaching delivery in the way that the original orator intended. Creating these conditions and modelling truly brilliant reading are among teachers' many magical powers.

Equally so, the performative nature of rhetoric should not be ignored, and it brings us astutely back to Britton's musing, 'reading floats on a sea of talk'.[8] Both the act of engaging in discussion around a text, and forming a rhetorical response that can be performed, whether it be speech or poetry, makes explicit to students the very potency that rhetoric holds in our societal tapestry. When forming a rhetoric sequence of study, teachers and leaders should seek to strive for balance in form, practice and application of these forms. Above all, they should practise giving learners the opportunity to deliver rhetoric in the way it was intended. Nothing is more despairing than a speech sat neglected on a page! Taking the time to celebrate and evaluate this work as a collective is deeply powerful for developing students' mental models of rhetoric as part of their real-world, lived experience.

And finally, to writing. The new writing framework (Department for Education, 2025) provides guidance for schools in England on how to build a progression model for the procedure of writing in schools. These all act as a foundational knowledge base for students to be able to engage critically with both their own writing or speech and that of others. The framework makes reference to rhetoric as follows:

In Key Stage 2, pupils should be taught to discuss and draw on existing texts as part of planning their writing, but these should be separate from the books read for pleasure in class. This continues into Key Stage 3: the national curriculum requires pupils to draw on 'knowledge of literary and rhetorical devices from their reading and listening to enhance the impact of their writing'.[9]

This reinforces the requirement for rhetoric to feature as a staple component of the taught curriculum but means that we should treat the rhetorical framework and devices with the same level of importance that we do with grammar, or vocabulary acquisition, or descriptive devices in narratives or fiction texts. To employ rhetorical structure or devices within writing, students must identify them, use them, refine and redraft them and reach a level of mastery in their own text composition where they can recognise, name and explain the effect of rhetorical devices. Perhaps it's time for the simile and metaphor to move over a little.

The role of enrichment to ensure both beauty and utility of rhetoric in schools

Before we turn to the principles of curriculum design, the substance of rhetoric in schools must not just be considered within academic study, but of the lived experience of pupils as well. If we are to use the curriculum to demonstrate its academic value, we must also provide experiences for children to test out this knowledge, honing their delivery and execution of rhetoric within a climate that cultivates this safely for practice and mastery over time.

Schools have an abundance of levers through which they can bring rhetoric to life for students. For example, from debating clubs to speech clubs, where students present compelling 'talk for a minute' speeches to peers; school councils, where students act as representatives of their year group or house, to the student editorial magazine, performance poetry and spoken word contests. Students are not just inducted into a level of understanding through the taught content of the curriculum, but they require the opportunities to see themselves as writers and orators in their own right. Such provisions are possible in synergy with teaching rhetoric, and will often evolve through the curiosity of students. All enrichment opportunities that feed the curriculum and provide tangible, real-life moments of bringing learning to life.

- Establish a sense of progression through revisiting and building upon acquisition, particularly through comparative study as a means to analyse and evaluate texts
- Consider a balanced approach of reading, writing and speaking when curating a knowledge base for rhetoric
- Explore an enrichment offer that acts as an embellishment to the taught component of rhetoric in your school setting.

In summary:

- **Rhetoric equips pupils to judge, interpret and construct communication**, enabling them to read nuance, recognise manipulation and become confident, critical communicators across contexts
- **A clear curriculum intention for rhetoric is essential**, positioning it as a domain of knowledge, skill and understanding that supports wider literacy, critical thinking and the school's literacy strategy more broadly
- **Critical thinking develops primarily through domain-specific knowledge and guided practice**, with rhetoric providing a structured route from comprehension to evaluation through appeals, argument structures and refutation
- **High-quality texts and explicit teaching of rhetorical appeals and devices** (*ethos*, *logos*, *pathos* and core techniques) form the backbone of a rigorous rhetoric curriculum, supported by careful, age-appropriate text selection
- **Rhetoric offers an efficient, coherent pedagogical framework**. It unites literacy, critical thinking and critical literacy and provides a progression pathway from recognising persuasive techniques to mastering the construction and deconstruction of arguments

Notes

1 Willingham, D.T. (2008) 'Critical thinking: Why is it so hard to teach?', *Arts Education Policy Review*, 109, 4, 21–32 http://dx.doi.org/10.3200/AEPR.109.4.21-32
2 Willingham, D.T. (2019) 'How to teach critical thinking', *Education: Future Frontiers*, *1*, 1, 1–17.
3 For more on this, we recommend reading Barnett, S.M. and Ceci, S.J. (2002) 'When and where do we apply what we learn?: A taxonomy for far transfer', *Psychological Bulletin*, *128*, 4, 612.
4 Known as 'language about language' (Stevens and Bean 2007: 25).
5 Also referred to as 'analysis and genesis' by Newlands and Murphy (2010: 18).
6 These rhetorical techniques occur commonly in Latin literature, and examples of their use are explained in the glossary on pages ix and x.
7 For more interesting reading on how students move from concrete, simple knowledge to more abstract, systematic and powerful knowledge within a specific discipline, we recommend reading Winch, C. (2013) 'Curriculum design and epistemic ascent', *Journal of Philosophy of Education*, 47, 1, 128–146, https://doi.org/10.1111/1467-9752.12006
8 Britton, J. (1970) *Language and learning*, University of Miami Press, Coral Gables, FL.
9 Department for Education (2025) *The Writing Framework*. Accessed online at https://assets.publishing.service.gov.uk/media/68bec95444fd43581bda1c86/The_writing_framework_092025.pdf.

5 Rhetoric across the curriculum

Why do we need to start with the curriculum when considering the revival of rhetoric?

The curriculum is the very bedrock of education. With a well-designed curriculum, teachers and leaders are able to set out their vision, ambition and intention to all key stakeholders for how they define education for young people in their setting, why it matters and how they will endeavour to deliver on that through the substance of what is taught. Curriculum is a highly contestable aspect of education, and when such a debate reaches school leaders' desks, to some degree, the conclusion to the argument has already been decided. However, the ongoing tensions between our interpretation of what education should set out to achieve and the enacted curriculum that a school should seek to deliver often demonstrate that this debate is far from a conclusion. The definition of curriculum through a philosophical lens is to some extent motivated by political intervention; however, such debates endure, and this will inevitably have an impact upon the curricular intentions of the classroom teacher, as well as the student experience.

Part A of this book outlined the heritage, legacy and evolution of rhetoric as a vital part of human existence. Part B of this book aims to support you with what comes next, so that you can consider how you prepare young people for the world they find themselves in today. However, in order to implement the knowledge, skills and understanding of rhetoric as part of our overall offer, we must first consider the quality of the curriculum, how we shape this, and the place that rhetoric occupies in the learning experiences of young people in our schools.

To do so, let's begin with curriculum; what it does, and where it sometimes flounders, so that we might think about where teaching rhetoric as a thread might support some of the common problems of practice.

DOI: 10.4324/9781003409069-7

Yes, but what do we mean by curriculum?

Put ten teachers in a room and ask them to define the word 'curriculum', and we might be there for a little while. Curriculum is contentious (especially so for English, History and the Arts – we find it impossible to agree) – but there is merit in establishing a bit of universality to be able to consider the role that rhetoric might play in curriculum design and development. So, see this as a series of provocations for you to draw together your own definition.

For the purpose of educational impact, agreeing on a definition of curriculum presents challenges; key theorists are unable to agree upon the purpose of education, and these have been distorted once translated to school settings. Whilst Arnold posits that curriculum is 'the best of what has been thought and known' (Arnold 1873), this has resulted in Arnold's statement being translated as a claim for the literary canon, or traditionalism, where the quotation has lost context. Bernstein asserts that schools should seek to encourage students to 'think the unthinkable and not yet thought'[1] (Bernstein 2000), his leading argument is placed primarily within the realms of language. He provides a framework within which students can access knowledge that, at first, might feel alien when placed within subject domains. The framework enables them to reach the point where they can make sense of the world without the formality of asserting, 'this is maths!' or 'this is a period of history!' to make sense of it all.

For many of us working in or across schools with a number of children from disadvantaged backgrounds, curriculum serves those who need and deserve it the most. We might claim that curriculum is a vehicle for social justice. Counsell acknowledges that curriculum 'is all about power' (Counsell 2018), because such decisions are perhaps most likely lying in policymakers' and school leaders' hands. This abnegation of power is sometimes experienced by leaders and teachers, where the direction of what should be taught in schools is often not determined by those who undertake this work every day in classrooms. The Curriculum and Assessment Review Final report (Francis, 2025) urges the Department for Education to make further improvements in this regard. We know that curriculum needs to serve young people from disadvantaged backgrounds; we know that, in some cases, it fails to do so, and teachers are committed to improving this.

Martin Robinson argues 'the main job of a school isn't just to help pupils get high grades, it is to help provide meaning. This is the function of the curriculum'.[2] Because, the greatest gift that a school can provide to a child is a strong set of results, but it shouldn't be the process and journey through which we look at curriculum; it is a by-product of having access to a brilliant set of subject advocates (teachers), who prompt students to fall in love with their subjects. To do so, we must give forethought to that journey. And so, for the sake of simplicity, let us say that curriculum exists to ensure that teachers consider what they will teach, why and how it might look during episodes of learning and how these feed into a macro-level plan. After all, Wiliam asserts that, 'teachers create and develop curriculum every day'.[3]

- What is your definition for the curriculum?
- What is your curriculum aspiring to do?
- For leaders: is this a shared definition and understanding? How do you know?

A note on curriculum design

If we are to consider the opportunity offered by the curriculum as a social entitlement for all, then we might wish to consider the way in which curriculum is designed to deliver value. This will help us to explore rhetoric's role here. We turn now to common assumptions held about the curriculum, before shifting focus from theory to implementation.

The first assumption is that a well-designed curriculum considers the role of knowledge and skills: knowledge acquisition as a powerful mechanism for students to build firm foundations to apply, practise and develop fluency (skills) that draw on this perpetual building of, and returning to, knowledge over time. Hirsch asserts that knowledge is a social right, and that fear of knowledge has previously acted as an obstacle for schools that might feel ill-equipped to teach the 'best' to students who will inevitably find it challenging (Hirsch, Kett and Trefil 1988).[4] Yet, knowledge is far from the cold, rote learning we may have been led to believe: knowledge is a preface to skill, as skill cannot be taught in a vacuum. Author of *Seven Myths About Education* (2014), Daisy Christodoulou asserted,

> We've created a false dichotomy. Skill is bound up with knowledge. Skills are domain specific. You can't play chess unless you've learned the moves. I absolutely agree that the end of education is skilled, creative, critical individuals who can sift evidence. It's a question of how we get there.[5]

Our role is to induct students into a level of understanding that enables them to pursue either an academic study or simply a lifetime exploration of curiosity in the subject itself. Bringing together knowing and applying is therefore crucial to such an induction. And knowledge is generative: the more knowledge a student has, the more they will be able to learn as a result, but the more they will be able to critique the world for themselves. Muller refers to this concept as 'epistemological access'[6] (Muller 2014); enabling learners to consider not just what they are taught, but their interpretation of the content. How does this change or affirm their view or the views of others?

Therefore, to teach rhetoric well, we should consider what we want students to know, the technicalities of this knowledge and how far removed it is from the core curriculum, and how we integrate it in a meaningful and purposeful way.

The second assumption is that there are vertical and horizontal considerations for curriculum design: through knowledge acquisition and the application of this knowledge. By vertical, we mean the subject-specific lens where rhetoric might apply, and by horizontal, we mean the way in which principles or features of rhetoric could be applied across the whole-school curriculum.

For instance, a child will acquire knowledge regarding *ethos*, *logos* and *pathos* that enables them to analyse speech and the use of language to persuade. Or in Religious Studies, they might consider Augustine's argument that Christians must be capable of applying rhetoric to spread their faith and mitigate against the competing rhetoric of others. This would be considered a vertical design choice and implementation. In horizontal application, we might see specific frameworks deployed which make explicit use of rhetorical techniques as part of a whole-school oracy initiative. The construction of an argument therefore utilises the speaker as an expert, draws on other data and evidence to further assert this, but with an awareness of the audience's biases and objections that they must overcome by cultivating a human connection.

In earlier chapters of this book, we explored the universal nature of teaching children the principles of rhetoric, but there also are subject-specific implications (and advantages) of doing so. It is therefore worthy to think of the curriculum content as an opportunity to build children' s knowledge and awareness of rhetoric in three layers: taught as an explicit domain in its own right; taught through a set of shared principles across a school setting that very quickly become distinctive to subjects, but also the role that rhetoric as a discipline acts as an 'overlay' to subject and phase-specific curriculum, and how that acts as a journey of progression. None is more or less valuable than the next. When well executed, these enable children to recognise the role that language possesses to organise and uphold specific social groups across multiple places in history and society.

School leaders and teachers should therefore look at the place of rhetoric within their wider curriculum, aware of the broader context of knowledge and skills in both the proposed and the existing offer. This will be explored in greater depth in Chapter 6, when we consider implementation, but we would certainly ask that leaders evaluate the current curriculum ahead of implementing rhetoric. This will ensure that the vision holds strong, there is a clear sense of progression, and most importantly, everyone enacting the curriculum can define these accordingly.

- What is your current evaluation practice for the curriculum?
- How would you currently describe the quality of the curriculum?
- Which area is currently most fragile and why?
- What will you therefore prioritise when considering the addition of rhetoric?

Posing the problem of practice

With these considerations in mind, teachers and leaders should be prompted to consider two key principles. The first is to what extent there is intentionality in the explicit teaching of speaking, writing and reading as an overlay of the core curriculum offer. Do subject or phase leaders and teachers feel confident, emboldened by the necessary knowledge and expertise to bring this to life in the classroom?

The second is more complex but equally essential, and concerns the place (and indeed, the leverage) that rhetoric holds within the curriculum. When executed well, does knowledge of rhetoric work symbiotically with the development of specific skills to support young people to read, write and speak well? These are two provocations that Part B of this book attempts to answer. If you are a teacher, subject or phase leader or indeed someone leading a school or group of schools, you might start your thinking here.

However, curriculum is not a perception, but the lived reality of what young people learn every day. If we are to take the living, breathing entity of teaching component upon component as our most faithful model for this, then it is only right that we consider the way in which we teach young people to think, talk and engage with the concept of rhetoric as part of their fundamental right. Whether it rings true with you as a reader that curriculum should pursue social justice or disregard it altogether for something of more purity, the act of talk sits at the heart of the human condition. And so, we must teach it, and teach it well.

- How are knowledge and skills mapped out and balanced across your curriculum vision and how are they enacted in classrooms?
- How is this designed to ensure skills are not taught in a vacuum?
- What do we want young people to know and be able to do?
- How might this look for the taught study of rhetoric?

Why rhetoric, why now?

We would like to hope that your curiosity as a reader began when picking up this book, and that Part A of the book went some way towards building the educational, civic and social case for rhetoric. It is pivotal that children understand the world in which they live, and the historical and social influences that the use of rhetoric has had in shaping change. Students must therefore be taught through the core curriculum – not just what rhetorical language looks like and where or why it might come to be prevalent, but also how to equip themselves with persuasion to move as experts within the wider world.

The case for rhetoric is not new, yet it is important to draw on more recent educational literature that makes this case relevant to the taught curriculum. A deep understanding and use of language is possible for school pupils and it should not just be a bolt-on in their educational experience.

We start with the current educational climate and the value of rhetoric as part of that emerging narrative.

The 2022 Ofsted Research Review for English included a whole section on the importance of rhetoric:

> The discipline of rhetoric can provide pupils with insight into how spoken language is used by writers and orators.
>
> For older pupils, the discipline of rhetoric can give an insight into how writers and orators use spoken language. Pupils can learn how spoken language is constructed and produced, and the connections between words, sentences and whole texts or in speech, from individual utterances to dialogues and speeches. Pupils can learn about the meanings and nuances of the spoken word, the craft of a writer or speaker, and the ways in which spoken language conveys, explores and manipulates meaning. They can grasp the role and effect of rhetorical devices, the range of registers and social contexts of spoken language in use, the interplay of speaking, reading and writing, the artistry of spoken language and the knowledge and skills that underpin that artistry.

Becky Francis' (2025) final report of the Curriculum and Assessment Review recognised the importance of 'speaking, listening, and communication, including verbal as well as other forms of non-written communication, such as sign language, non-verbal and Alternative and Augmentative Communication (AAC)'. These were identified as having a direct influence on a wide range of life outcomes, including learning, employment, productivity, and psychological and physical health. The curriculum provides frequent opportunities for pupils to practise, refine and apply their spoken language knowledge and skills.

The report recommended the introduction of a new national oracy framework to give guidance to teachers and support good practice, In its response, the Government committed to do this. Francis also recommended that the Government should provide evidence-led guidance on curriculum and pedagogical adaptation for children and young people with Special Educational Needs and Disabilities (SEND). The Government response included a commitment to develop evidence-led resources to support teachers in making sure that the oracy curriculum is accessible to all children and young people, including those with SEND.

While rhetoric is not mentioned directly, we celebrate the extent to which Becky Francis appears to have been influenced by the Independent Oracy Education Commission's report (2024). This report outlines that 'the study of speech and debate (perhaps through the study of rhetoric)' is a key aspect of education. Moreover, the report provides explicit guidance to educators and academics regarding the three key overarching components to establish a shared language for oracy in the education space:

a. *Learning to talk, listen and communicate:* the development of children's speaking, listening and communication skills

b. *Learning through talk, listening and communication:* the use of talk or dialogue to foster and deepen children's learning

c. *Learning about talk, listening and communication:* building knowledge and understanding of speaking, listening and communication in its many contexts[7]

Rhetoric teaches young people the foundational knowledge of talk. Via rhetorical learning, students recognise the role that rhetoric plays in both fiction and non-fiction texts to develop meaning. The report goes on to state that 'oracy is a curricular goal in its own right',[8] and in order for schools to realise this goal, there must be a coherent strategy and the relevant tools to bring it to fruition.

Furthermore, specific subjects call for the same. The 2024 Ofsted subject report for English entitled *Telling the Story*[9] highlights findings from the lived experiences schools where the curriculum for written and spoken language was effective. But it also highlights where things were not working (often the result of complex tasks being introduced as part of the curriculum too early, or insufficient time allocated to build the necessary knowledge and skills) undermining a student's ability to apply learning to a written task. For example, a student may be able to analyse the technical language used within a text, but within reading for meaning, may miss the nuances of manipulation that an understanding of rhetoric would bring to embellish this analysis and provide a more evaluative lens. In addition, the subject report shared that pupils needed increased opportunities to reflect on the way in which expert speakers communicate. In the same way that a model text might support the practice and mastery of writing, a range of speeches for different contexts and with different intentions would provide students with the opportunity to practise and refine their own approach when speaking and listening. Yet, the report specified the possible pitfalls for schools to be wary of when considering this:

> However, decisions about the explicit teaching of spoken language are often left to individual teachers. Many schools have recently introduced spoken language assessments in key stage 3 in response to a perceived lack of confidence that pupils displayed when they came to do their spoken language assessment. Pupils are therefore being given more opportunities to practise speaking in different contexts and for different purposes. However, although these opportunities have increased, the schools have not clearly defined what pupils specifically need to know and practise doing to get better at speaking.[10]

It is why, when setting out on the exciting journey of bringing rhetoric to the school and subject curriculum offer, it must start with curriculum. Variance in classrooms where teachers are working with a mixed or unclear definition of rhetoric will be inevitably and unknowingly working against one another. In addition, the Ofsted report (2024) captures the distinction between curriculum and exam specification: the introduction of the speaking and listening component as a separate certification to the reformed 2015 English Language GCSE, coupled with the loss of more technical aspects of language study such as David Crystal's language change, or transcript analysis has led to some schools increasing the time students speak or listen, so that students speak or listen more effectively. Yet, without naming excellence in this or defining what knowledge and expertise are required to become expert at it, progression becomes a little tricky. The Ofsted report captures what's working:

> Where schools have identified the components that pupils need to be taught in relation to spoken language ... these schools have also recognised the important relationship between spoken language, reading and writing.[11]

And it is understandable to recognise why, in schools, we might find it challenging to turn this into a tangible strategy, when, as a sector, we do not hold universal definitions for numerous aspects of educational delivery. Even as we write this chapter, we select words such as 'oracy', 'rhetoric', 'literacy' with the caution they deserve, with the knowledge that these, along with 'curriculum', do not hold the same meanings for you as a reader, in the school where you work now, or the schools where you have worked previously. The legacy lexicon is somewhat against us. Yet it is an important pursuit for us to take together, because young people's learning relies on it. By drawing down quickly from centrally stored documents or esoteric terms that sit in papers from academics about what the citizens of the future should know, do or understand, we continue to attempt to bring rhetoric to life in schools. We sketch what such innovation might look like for you in your classroom or beyond.

A solitary teacher cannot move forward with implementation because not only will other learners not in their classroom fail to benefit, but there may also emerge a disconnect in the language and value of rhetoric as a result of their solo efforts. And so, curriculum is where we place the study of rhetoric, because it is right and just that students are given the dedicated time within their educational offer to think hard about the knowledge taught, articulate these thinking processes out loud with expert teachers and apply this to their own creations. Furthermore, it avoids the lethal mutations that we sometimes see as a result of implementation without high-quality training, investment, opportunity and evaluation with the teachers driving it.

- Rhetoric provides a tangible way to teach spoken and written language effectively
- It is crucial for leaders and teachers to clearly define rhetoric and what it means to be an expert through naming knowledge, skills and understanding of rhetoric

- The most effective schools will consider the relationship between spoken language, written language and reading
- Ensuring a place for rhetoric in the curriculum ensures we avoid variance in quality for learners educational experience

A cautionary note on subject specificity

Whilst senior leaders have an overview of wider school policy, this needs to be sympathetic to individual subject disciplines when considering the inclusion of rhetoric. Schools will make strategic decisions regarding how they wish to begin the early stages of implementation.

School improvement is often unsuccessful when policies or initiatives ask subjects to comply with generic strategies that inadvertently manipulate the discipline. This approach often removes the 'dignity of the thing'[12] by attempting to appropriate 'what works' in one subject and applying it to all. We all benefit from seeing good models in our own schools or indeed elsewhere, but these need to take account of the distinct differences between subjects. The best way to design and deliver the teaching of rhetoric for one subject is likely to differ from another. Equally, if we attempt to constrain the curriculum to a cross-subject scheme of work template, we risk doing disservice to the subject through our attempt to bend and manipulate it to fit into neat tables and boxes. Streamlining subjects down to 'one size fits all' is naive to both the subject and those who serve it; the curriculum cannot be tamed. Rhetoric fits the same requisites. Leaders and teachers should consider this in both curriculum design and implementation (which is covered in the Chapter 6). Of any successful initiatives, 50% is in the substance, and 50% is in the way colleagues are supported to implement it.

Therefore, the way we measure success needs to be reframed as something fit for purpose: a methodology that recognises that curriculum must be designed, undertaken, delivered and evaluated with a sensitive touch – bespoke to the subject itself.

How do I construct a curriculum of rhetoric in my school?

Evaluate what is already there

Before a consideration of where things 'fit', let's take a look at what is already present and already working. An initial provocation with senior and subject leaders, or indeed a subject team, may centre around the degree to which there is a sense of the following:

- Do we teach students rhetorical structure and devices when undertaking analysis, writing in independent work or speaking exercises, and how would we describe the quality of this?
- Do we teach students the distinction between argument and rhetorical technique, and the elevation that rhetoric brings to argument or persuasion?

- What texts do we use to understand, analyse and evaluate rhetorical techniques with students, and what is the quality of these? How were they selected?
- What task design is used when students apply this knowledge (opinion editorial? speeches?), and to what degree is this fitting to both student age and subject content?
- Are students taught to evaluate the strength of an argument, including the use of logical fallacies?
- How common are our approaches as a team or school when looking at our current practice?

This discussion as a team will also enable you individually and collectively to consider your own knowledge base ahead of beginning the exciting work of making changes to the curriculum. This is a fundamental part of the process; looking at implementation and professional learning priorities provides a foundation for identifying and making next steps.

Ascertain a shared language and common approaches in curriculum enactment

When Kat works with schools and trusts to develop their curriculum, it often transpires that there is one of two challenges preventing them from integrating rhetoric as part of their curriculum offer:

- They do not have a shared language and understanding of the knowledge, skills and understanding that they wish for teachers to teach and students to access
- There are legacy approaches that contradict one another, resulting in variable approaches and preventing students from building a sense of familiarity over time so that they can become experts

A shared language

A useful exercise, individually or as a team, is to first consider what it is that students need to understand, analyse, apply and evaluate using rhetoric in a specific subject and capture this as a collaborative task. For instance, this might be the particular techniques employed by writers and a specific structure to use when forming a piece of rhetorical writing. It may be a discussion where a team compiles a succinct list of key orators over history and the modern day that they feel would both expose their students to new knowledge, but also enable them to feel represented in the curriculum. Building up a body of work that centres around the question: 'what do we, this team, for this subject, in this school, for these students mean by rhetoric?', is a brilliant starting point (Figure 5.1).

Year 8 - Knowledge Organiser – Rhetoric

Rhetorical language is how we form our arguments, views and put across our ideas in a convincing way. This unit will explore several great figures in history and consider the different ways rhetoric has influenced our world today.

The Aristotelian Triad

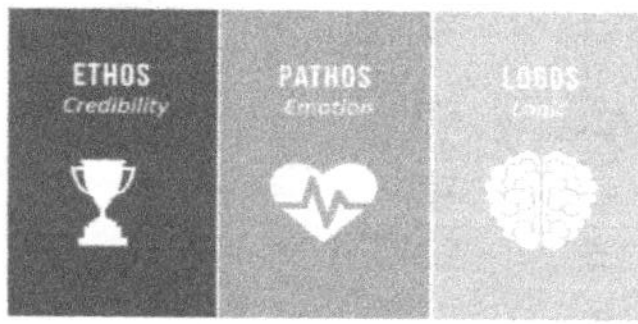

Aristotle outlined that an effective persuasive argument must contain these three elements to be successful.

What is rhetoric often used within and for what purpose?

Speech	Speaking formally to an audience. A speech will open using a powerful image, anecdote or pose a question to the audience. The most effective speeches end with a powerful message.	**Action**	The purpose of a piece of writing could be to demand that action be taken to change or stop something happening.
Poem	Poems are a form of literature that can be used to share ideas or opinions about society. Polemic poetry is poetry used to create a debate or highlight problem.	**Injustice**	If something feels unjust, it means it is unfair or undeserved. It ay be that a person has chosen to use rhetoric to highlight the poor treatment of a particular group of people.
Article	A news article discuss current or recent news. This can be general news that will appeal to most readers, or on a specific topic for a particular audience.	**Motivation**	Motivating people is to make them feel enthusiastic or driven to believe an idea, or to take action. It may be that the speaker or writer is trying to give people hope or an optimistic outlook.
Letter	A written form of communication, this are usually a formal way of outlining and issue, applying for a job or writing in response to share your opinion.	**Change**	Sometimes, speakers or writers are highlighting key issues in such a way that they provide ways in which these issues could be resolved. They will provide a range of ways that people can solve the problem within the speech, letter, article or poem.

Key Vocabulary:

Alliteration	Repeating the same sound at the start of consecutive words.	**Emotive language**	Words or phrases that encourage the reader or audience to feel a particular emotion.	**Pathos**	Pathos is the emotional influence of the speaker on the audience. Its goal is to make the audience feel something.
Anecdote	A short amusing or interesting story about a real incident or person.	**Ethos**	Credibility. "You should believe my argument because you believe *me.*" or perhaps "...believe *in me.*"	**Polemic**	A written debate or dispute.
Anaphora	Starting each sentence with the same words.	**Hyperbole**	Exaggeration to emphasise a point or idea.	**Proof**	Evidence to support your ideas or opinions.
Antithesis	Direct opposites.	**Hypophora**	A question followed by the answer.	**Purpose**	The reason the writer is writing.
Dialysis	'Don't do this, do that.' Presenting an alternative argument.	**Injustice**	If something is unfair.	**Rhetorical question**	A question that doesn't require an answer, but is instead used to make a point.
Direct address	Use of a proper noun (you) to address the audience.	**Logos**	Using logic and reasoning as your appeal: facts and figures.	**Tricolon**	Use of a list of three, or repetition of something three times, to emphasise a point.

Key rhetoric speakers throughout history

Aristotle: The original expert of rhetoric.	Aspasia	Cicero	Elizabeth I	Sojourner Truth	Emmeline Pankhurst	Winston Churchill	Gandhi	Martin Luther King	Malala Yousafzai	Michelle Obama	Barack Obama	Emma Watson

Figure 5.1 Knowledge Organiser for Rhetoric.

Reviewing legacy approaches and ensuring fitness for purpose

It may be that students have been taught writing through other means previously in your setting, and that the employment of rhetorical devices or use of texts where authors do so is not currently a feature within your curriculum. However, more often than not, rhetorical writing and reading for persuasion features as a legacy item on English curriculum planning, with certain acronyms that attempt to support the construction of crafting a piece of writing for students. There may already exist a selection of texts that has been collated over time to provide breadth through text form – speeches, advertisements and so forth – or with a similar level of reading accessibility.

When beginning this process of curriculum evaluation, it is worth considering the specific techniques that we would like learners to be able to use masterfully, and the potential acronyms which could reduce the cognitive demand for students. Martin Robsinson captures this astutely here in his observation of how codification impacts knowledge acquisition for students:

> It seemed to us that pupils were getting the grades in theatre studies as they manipulated the 'symbols' (the quotes, examples, 'criteria' hitting sentences) without understanding the subject. They had low level knowledge that worked for exams but not for their subject knowledge.[13]

For example, whilst DAFOREST and AFOREST[14] (and such like) attempt to codify rhetorical devices and make them identifiable to students, they are challenging to recall and apply in practice, especially when considering the intention, purpose and effectiveness of specific techniques when used to write well. For instance, a child may know that the F in the acronym is facts, but this will not enable them to know how best to craft words and sentences to integrate facts compellingly. We often ask a child to recall what the acronym stands for. Do we wish for children to read, write and speak well, or to recall the acronym without the knowledge behind it to then develop expertise?

With the best of intentions, the tool becomes a cognitive barrier to enable the child to apply this to their work, and they will invariably avoid using it as a result. Equally, when considering writing frameworks, it is worth approaching such a task with professional curiosity, and a shared endeavour to land on something that all teachers will use. This means that the teacher in Year 3 is benefitting the teacher in Year 4 or 5 in building familiarity for students in relation to their curriculum experience – but with parameters that it is strong enough to support student construction, but not constrained enough that it hinders excellence as students become experts in their own right.

Equally, the models of rhetoric that are placed in front of children will provide valuable exemplification of, lead to how, if questioned, they might define excellent use of rhetoric in written or spoken communication later on. Teams and teachers selecting such models may wish to spend time deliberating whether the selection is currently in place, or, if starting from scratch, the new selection proposed will subsequently support students when creating their own works or undertaking their own analysis and evaluation of excellence.

- What is our definition of excellence for teaching rhetoric?
- What are the knowledge, skills and understanding required to become a student expert?
- What shared tools and models might we use to achieve this?

What do I need to consider as a school or subject leader?

Once you have evaluated the current offer, it is critical that the collective knowledge of the team around the curriculum is also evaluated. Normalising the fact that rhetoric study is not yet commonplace on the curriculum, but that there is a growing body of evidence that supports it to be present, will enable this conversation with colleagues. There is a common misconception that teachers should possess all knowledge to teach all things: the historian should have taught world, national and local level history in its entirety; the linguist has taught all languages to all students of all ages; the literature teacher has read all of the books. Discussing the organisational readiness of a team and what knowledge enhancement they need will help to eradicate this unhelpful narrative that we are experts in all things, and again, will support implementation.

This may involve an exploration of curriculum theory more broadly: discussing the existence of concepts or big ideas for students to consider over a long-term period of study as a means to progression, and how knowledge and skills are developed over time. It may be of merit to explore the sequence of the existing curriculum and engage in a discussion to reach a rationale and how one segment of curriculum supports knowledge acquisition in later study. It can also be useful to consider the role that assessment plays in progression over time through a sampling of the curriculum content studied. Such discussions will aid leaders and teachers to make decisions regarding what the collective ambition is but also what the next steps are in the short, medium and long terms.

What do I need to consider as a teacher?

If you are reading this as a classroom teacher and want to explore rhetoric as part of your curriculum, consider the curriculum that you currently teach. Where is there existing strength, and how have you reached this conclusion? Which aspect of the curriculum would lend itself to teaching rhetoric in a way that feels logical and sensible? With what you now know, where feels like an ideal place to begin to develop students' thinking around rhetoric?

We often think about curriculum development and evolution as an overhaul: ripping out a carpet to replace it with one that feels newer, more exciting, yet somewhat unfamiliar. There is much to be gained, we think, by thinking of it as an embellishment of what has been in place before, so that instead of an overhaul, it is to focus on one particular corner and tidy that up a bit. This might be when teaching Pope Urban II's speech at Clermont that launched the Crusades in History to analyse and evaluate its influence, or studying Attenborough's closing words on Planet Earth around conservation in Geography. It may be trialling a specific framework for writing using rhetoric in Year 7 across two or three subjects, and capturing clear success criteria to be able to evaluate the success of this. Small, succinct evaluations of curriculum can be easily measured and give us early signs of reassurance that such an approach is benefitting the young people we teach. In addition, it makes the process manageable and (we think) really enjoyable as a teacher!

- Identify the improvement that you wish to see in the curriculum design and enactment in the classroom.
- Consider a collaborative multi-disciplinary approach to see how staff knowledge of rhetoric develops over time.
- Consider the professional starting point and opportunities for learning of those staff involved in curriculum changes.

For more on purposeful curriculum design more broadly, we signpost Kat's earlier book *Symbiosis* co-written with Claire Hill,[15] where we attend to some of the knowledge, opportunities and challenges offered by curriculum development in schools. At this stage, we bring in the experiences of colleagues who have grappled with bringing rhetoric to life in their school settings. They explain how rhetoric plays a role in the delivery of education for their young people, the process of implementation where rhetoric features within their curriculum, and the learning lessons gained as a result.

Here, we might consider the way in which this would manifest through different subject disciplines as part of the taught curriculum.

We have seen already that English has an important role to play in providing a vehicle for the composition of communication and the practice of rhetorical invention and performance.

Aside from English, we consider that important contributions can also be made by History, Religious, Moral and Philosophical Studies (RMPS), Citizenship/Politics and Media Studies. RMPS offers opportunities to critically analyse the beliefs, scriptures and sermons of diverse faith groups, which may be written to persuade others to become followers. In this connection, students have plenty of opportunity to employ and develop critical thinking and critical literacy skills, as well as become increasingly aware of their role as citizens in a multi-faith world. Politics includes direct study and analysis of political life and can include the analysis of modern (and some historical) political speeches. It encourages students to probe their own considerations on the rights and responsibilities of citizens while expecting them to articulate their position competently. The ability to consider and ask difficult questions is a key feature of Modern Studies education (Maitles 2003) and here, the subject has a significant role to play in educating for democratic citizenship. Politics is located at an intersection of the curriculum – where communication studies and citizenship meet; it occupies space between the Humanities and the Social Sciences. This makes it a very useful and cross-curricular subject for the delivery of rhetorical education. In its current form, it does not offer a sufficiently detailed study of language to be able to teach exclusively about rhetoric, hence our recommendation for an inter-disciplinary approach which combines the study of politics and citizenship with historical speeches.

Film and Media Studies, too, offer possible input to the teaching and learning of rhetoric in schools and colleges. They prepare students to see beyond the way events are reported in the media or reinterpreted by Hollywood to distinguish fact from fiction, truth from make-believe. Given how digitally and technologically advanced our society has become, Media Studies is perhaps in a stronger curricular position for delivering rhetorical education to students, as it is not generally criticised, as Latin is, for being out of date and irrelevant to young people today. Welch (1999: 101) notes that the high number of 'HUTs, households using television, and the machine's ubiquity has changed rhetoric'. Television has become so heavily implicated in people's acquisition of language that there ought to be training in how to be effective decoders of the communication content and style, seen and heard, on television. Media Studies can go some way to providing 'training in the grammar, vocabulary and ideology of digital communication' (Welch 1999: 134), especially important given the tendency for the communication 'power mongers of post-Fordism to intellectually colonise our citizenry' (Welch 1999: 189). Without the capacity and ability for critical judgement, the television companies, social media moguls and producers will narcotise us into believing unquestioningly and consuming what they so imprecisely call 'information' and 'content'. Communication disseminated digitally is often rhetorical and involves persuasion; thus there exists an inherently rhetorical relationship between social and literary analysis and communication technologies. Welch (1999: 179) uses a pair of powerful metaphors which show the intersection of rhetoric, media and technology with captivating imagery,

> if television offers a Niagara Falls of rhetorical artefacts, both graphic and spoken (and both based on writing), then the digital world offers an Atlantic Ocean of rhetorical artefacts and performances, also written, graphic and spoken.

Through Media Studies, students can discover that cultures are composed of their rhetorics, and online technologies are at the centre of our current culture. To be cyberliterate, there is a need to go beyond merely being a user. Learners need to become active participants in the discussion, critiquing, challenging and anticipating how these technologies are designed, implemented and used (Gurak 2004: 191). We agree with Gurak (2004: 194) that the future of cyberliteracy needs to be critical, observant and activist; and we share her call for a curriculum that helps students understand and critically evaluate the rhetorical features of digital communication (Gurak 2004: xvi). Although a far cry from the study of rhetoric in Latin or Greek, the need for input from other subjects in the school curriculum is a result of the changing nature of rhetoric in contemporary society. This is no blight on classical languages, rather it is an indication that, as certain aspects of language and humanity stay the same, others change, and, as Ovid sagely advised (*Metamorphoses* 15.662), *'omnia mutantur nos et mutamur in illis'*, 'as all things change, we change with them'. The onus on educators, therefore, is to ensure that learners receive the best preparation each curricular area has to offer for the optimal study of rhetoric.

What, then, is rhetoric's optimal curricular position? The extent to which rhetoric ought to be viewed as a content-rich standalone subject in the curriculum is dependent to some degree on the current and future shape of educational policy. Currently, rhetoric makes only two appearances as a facet of high-quality English teaching (Ofsted 2022, 2024). It does not appear as a discrete subject in any curriculum in the UK's four nations, so it is difficult to imagine how such a scenario could arise except if this evolved from Francis' Curriculum and Assessment Review (2025) recommendations on a national oracy framework for all young people in all stages, and all subjects in England. Perhaps other devolved governments may then follow suit.

What might this look like in practice? Here we present two case studies written by practitioners who have embedded the teaching of rhetoric in their subject-specific classroom practice.

Case studies

CASE STUDY 1 Rhetoric Framework in Religious Education | Cristobal Rodriguez-Casado

Religious Education Context

Rhetoric can support high-quality Religious Education (RE) via its enrichment of the 'ways of knowing' aspect of RE and via the affinity of rhetoric and 'argument' in RE. These two foci can be strong vehicles for developing 'disciplinary'[16] knowledge in an RE curriculum.

The Ofsted Research Review in RE emphasises the importance of how substantive claims are made in RE and the specificity of knowledge around the 'claim making' process (Ofsted 2021:12). The Review makes clear that this process of claim making is particular to both the question and the content under study and also under-theorised[17] in the documentation of many RE curricula (Chan, Fancourt and Guilfoyle 2021).

Rhetoric can help to make this claim-making or 'argument' in RE specific to the discipline and, in doing so, to deepen students' appreciation for the disciplinary knowledge component of RE, and to understand and remember more of the curriculum. By developing students' appreciation of 'argument', their ability to think analytically improves in ways which are well suited to the discipline of RE.

Case Study Context

At the David Ross Education Trust, our Trust-wide subject community has begun to establish a trust-wide curriculum from Key Stage 3, which aims at developing epistemic literacy. We want students to be able to engage in the disciplines of theology, philosophy, history and the human sciences, and so our curriculum focusses on the concept of 'argument' in various contexts.

One part of our practice which marries well with the rhetorical focus on logos is the explicit teaching of descriptive terms and analytical concepts in analytic Philosophy. In Year 7, students learn to think of a philosophical argument as a series of 'premises' leading to a 'conclusion'. We explicitly teach specific Tier 3 vocabulary, such as 'premise' rather than 'point'. Students learn that a conclusion is 'what is shown by the argument' and that 'logic' is the rules of thinking that lead us from the premises to the conclusion. These descriptive terms enable students to look at arguments, including religious and non-religious arguments as structured claims, not just beliefs, which may or may not be 'true' based on 'good' or 'bad' arguments, which students may or may not already 'believe in'.

Analytical Practice

Once students are competent at describing the parts of an argument (we use various deliberate practice techniques), we introduce the terms 'valid' and 'sound'. Students are taught that a valid argument has a logical structure which makes sense; the conclusion is shown by the premises. We show how even arguments which have faulty conclusions can be valid in the structure of the argument. Students look at arguments such as this:

Socrates was a man

All men are mortal

Therefore Socrates was mortal

We show students examples of valid arguments which have obviously dubious conclusions.

All men are made of cheese

Socrates was a man

Therefore Socrates was made of cheese

Students are challenged to look at this argument and to describe it and then analyse it. Firstly, they have to label the parts and then state which part of the argument is faulty. Inevitably, they can see that the first premise, and therefore the conclusion, are false. They begin to understand that it is not just a valid structure that an argument needs, but also true premises. Students are then taught that a sound argument is valid and has true premises. Students then look at examples of several arguments and analyse using these categories: is the argument valid but not sound, or not valid and not sound, or is it a sound argument? Teachers can show various arguments and use questioning and responsive teaching to develop discussion, address terminological misconceptions and train students to apply these categories.

Students then meet the kalam cosmological argument which holds that everything that begins to exist has a cause, the universe began to exist, and therefore the universe has a cause. Students analyse this alongside an atheological argument based on Hume's problem of evil. With this grounding in place, students become more aware of the ways to criticise a conclusion by objecting to premises. So, rather than objecting or assenting to these arguments based on prior worldview commitment alone, there is an awareness of the need to deal with the truth of the premises and the validity of the logic. We build on valid/sound arguments, looking at the concepts of 'assumption', 'a priori' and 'a posteriori', 'deductive' and 'inductive' logic when meeting new arguments and dealing with metaphysical components of arguments (e.g., Hume on miracles). The discipline of philosophy becomes a vehicle for building epistemic literacy across Key Stage 3.

This emphasis on logos in argument has meant that students in RE are able to treat thinking as an 'extended project' and mitigate against 'early closure' to thinking in RE (Ashley 2005: 190). Through our in-house reflective practices and a research project (in collaboration with Culham St Gabriel's)[18] *we have seen that students are more aware of the reasons philosophers disagree on arguments and can see how a theist might look at the kalam as sound where as an atheist may look at the same argument and see it as valid but not sound. The discussion becomes about the adequacy of the premises.*

The focus on rhetorical logos has fed into the ongoing development of student disciplinary oracy, which we develop through a focus on disciplinary reasoning.

Oracy

We have developed oracy tasks with authentic and accountable student talk through a Talk Moves approach (particularly Turn and Talk with a focus on justification). We have developed multiple choice questions to use at the end of a learning sequence, which ask students to analyse an argument as valid but not sound, not valid or sound and then use logical chains of reasoning and Tier 3 vocabulary to justify their claims. We are applying some of these oracy opportunities in other areas of RE, such as theology (e.g., justifying interpretations based on texts) and, as we progress in the curriculum, sociology (e.g., justifying qualitative statements by sociologists and broadcasters based on quantitative data such as the 2021 census).

CASE STUDY 2 Design and Development of Rhetoric within the English Curriculum | Kat Howard

Refining the Curriculum for Deeper Disciplinary Thinking

Curriculum design is a process of constant refinement, shaped by emerging pedagogical research and the shifting demands of literacy in the wider world. We need to ensure that what is taught is as meaningful as possible. In recent years, English departments have increasingly recognised the limitations of legacy curriculum components that rely on surface-level engagement with persuasive writing. The plethora of techniques students were expected to master – ranging from alliteration to rhetorical questions – had become an unwieldy checklist, encouraging formulaic responses rather than deep rhetorical awareness. This prompted a reconsideration: rather than equipping students with an arbitrary collection of techniques, could we instead root their study in the principles of classical rhetoric, refining their analytical and compositional skills to be more purposeful, and therefore develop their expertise as a consequence?

The result was a redesigned unit of study that transitioned from a broad persuasive writing component to an explicit, rigorous exploration of rhetoric, underpinned by the Aristotelian triad of ethos, logos and pathos. This shift not only aligned more closely with the conceptual demands of English as a discipline but also provided students with a framework that has endured for centuries, shaping public discourse in times of protest, instability and change. This case study explores the rationale, design process and implementation of this rhetoric unit, demonstrating how intentional curriculum reform can elevate students' engagement with language as a tool of power and influence.

Case Study Context

This unit was part of a wider Key Stage 3 English curriculum review undertaken during the COVID-19 lockdown. The review was prompted by a series of legacy units within the curriculum where student attainment was less strong: a persuasive writing sequence and a travel writing sequence. This unit was developed and later used by Oak National Academy, an organisation leading a large-scale delivery of remote learning during the pandemic. Consequently, the curriculum content was accessed by thousands of children studying at home, and used later to support in-school learning.

A Clear Set of Principles for Excellence

The first stage of the redesign involved distilling the overwhelming number of persuasive techniques into a coherent, principle-driven approach. By grounding the study of rhetoric in the classical modes of appeal: ethos (credibility), logos (argument) and pathos (emotion), students were given an analytical lens that allowed them to assess how writers and speakers make strategic choices in response to their audience and purpose.

Once this foundational framework was established, a set of rhetorical devices was carefully selected, not as a checklist but as an interconnected toolkit that students could use to drive one or more of these three aspects effectively. For instance:

- *Ethos-driven devices: Use of personal anecdotes, references to expertise or authority, and direct engagement with counterarguments.*
- *Logos-driven devices: Logical structuring of arguments, use of statistics or factual evidence, and rhetorical questioning that anticipates audience objections.*
- *Pathos-driven devices:Vivid imagery, emotive language and strategic repetition for emphasis.*

By aligning techniques with their rhetorical function, students moved beyond arbitrary identification and towards a deeper understanding of how language operates in persuasive discourse. The impact of this shift was evident in students' ability to evaluate the effectiveness of a speaker's rhetoric and, crucially, in their ability to craft their own arguments with greater intentionality and impact.

Selecting Texts with Fidelity

The next step in the redesign was selecting a series of texts that exemplified rhetorical mastery with fidelity, ensuring that students engaged with rhetoric in its most authentic and effective forms. A key consideration was representation: texts needed to reflect a range of voices, spanning historical and contemporary contexts, while also offering variety in form – speeches, letters, polemic poetry and manifestos. The final selection included:

- *Elizabeth I's 'Tilbury Speech' (1588) – A demonstration of regal ethos, as Elizabeth strategically constructs herself as both a sovereign and a warrior alongside her troops.*
- *Sojourner Truth's 'Ain't I a Woman?' (1851) – A seminal speech that intertwines pathos and logos to dismantle racial and gendered oppression.*
- *Emmeline Pankhurst's 'Freedom or Death' (1913) – A rallying cry for suffrage, using defiance and repetition to galvanise an audience.*
- *Malala Yousafzai's UN Address (2013) – A testament to the power of rhetoric in activism, deploying personal narrative to establish ethos and stir pathos.*
- *Michelle Obama's 'When They Go Low, We Go High' (2016) – A contemporary speech that exemplifies rhetorical grace and moral authority.*

Each text was selected for its ability to demonstrate rhetoric in action, allowing students to see how figures across time have wielded language to challenge, inspire and persuade. The curation also reflected an intentional balance: female voices were centred, ensuring representation that historically has been marginalised in rhetorical studies (especially in the inherited legacy from the ancient world). Moreover, by including a range of forms, students encountered rhetoric not just as an abstract concept but as a lived and dynamic practice.

Designing Teacher Guidance

A well-designed curriculum is only as effective as its implementation. To ensure high-quality teaching of the unit, a series of key documents was developed to guide staff:

- *An overarching teaching guide: This document mapped out how a sequence might unfold over a term, providing a model of progression from initial conceptual understanding to sophisticated analytical and writing tasks. The final assessments were exemplified to establish clear success criteria, ensuring coherence between instruction and evaluation.*
- *A student workbook: This provided clear knowledge organisers outlining key rhetorical principles, with built-in opportunities for application and feedback. While structured, the workbook retained flexibility, allowing teachers to respond to the needs of their classes rather than adhering to rigid lesson scripts.*
- *A cohort-wide lecture to open the unit: The unit began with a masterclass, introducing students to rhetoric through an engaging, high-quality lecture that set the intellectual tone. This not only provided an overview of the key concepts but also modelled expert discourse, bridging the gap between prior learning and the new rhetorical framework content.*

The combination of structured guidance and space for responsive teaching ensured that students received a consistent, high-quality introduction to rhetoric while allowing teachers to adapt their approach for their individual classes.

Subject Knowledge as a Cornerstone

Recognising that effective curriculum change required investment in teacher expertise, professional development was embedded into the implementation process. This took several forms:

- *An expert crib sheet: A resource that signposted high-quality subject-specific professional development, including further reading, podcasts and multimodal materials. This enabled teachers to deepen their own understanding of rhetoric and its pedagogical applications.*
- *A dedicated curriculum walkthrough: A session designed to familiarise teachers with the texts, providing guidance on how to scaffold discussions, model analysis and support students in crafting their own rhetorical responses.*

By equipping teachers with both subject knowledge and pedagogical strategies, the unit was delivered with greater confidence and precision. The aim was not merely to teach students about rhetoric but to ensure that teachers felt empowered to teach it with intellectual rigour.

Exemplifying Curriculum Enactment

A defining moment in the project was the opportunity to contribute to the Oak National Academy 'Sprint' Project which was delivered at pace during the COVID-19 pandemic. This involved recording a series of lessons based on the rhetoric unit, providing a national model of how these concepts could be taught. The impact was twofold:

- *A ready-made set of exemplars: Teachers could draw on the recorded lessons to support their own instruction, ensuring that key ideas were delivered with clarity and expertise.*
- *Sustained impact beyond the initial implementation: Later in the academic year, these recorded lessons served as a resource for in-class observations and professional development, reinforcing consistency in the teaching of rhetoric.*

By integrating publicly available exemplars into professional development, the unit's reach extended beyond a single department, contributing to a broader discourse on how rhetoric can be meaningfully embedded into the curriculum.

Intentionality in Curriculum Design

The success of this rhetoric unit was not simply the result of content selection but rather of a carefully sequenced and intentional approach to curriculum design. By distilling persuasive writing into its essential rhetorical principles, selecting texts with fidelity, structuring teacher guidance for both clarity and flexibility, embedding professional development, and providing strong examples, the redesign ensured that rhetoric was taught with the depth and detail it deserved.

Beyond the immediate classroom impact, the shift towards a rhetoric-based approach has broader implications. It fosters a critical awareness of how language operates in moments of political and social upheaval, equipping students not just with the tools to analyse persuasive discourse, but with the ability to engage in it themselves.

In summary:

- **Rhetoric must be rooted in curriculum design**, beginning with clear definitions of curriculum, shared intentions at a strategic level and an understanding of how knowledge and skills interact within subjects on an inter-disciplinary level or as part of a wide school strategy
- **A case for rhetoric is growing nationally**, supported by the Oracy Education Commission, Ofsted subject reports and research reviews, and wider educational debate, highlighting rhetoric as essential for reading, writing, speaking and understanding the world

- **Implementation demands clarity to be successful**, requiring a shared language, common approaches, high-quality models, and deliberate progression, avoiding legacy practices, acronyms or inconsistent expectations that undermine expertise and conflate the meaning of what rhetoric is and why it matters
- **Rhetoric enhances subject-specific learning**, but leaders must avoid generic, one-size-fits-all approaches; instead, they need to consider disciplinary differences and design bespoke enactment and evaluation practices
- **Building a curriculum for rhetoric begins with evaluation**, identifying existing strengths, gaps and misconceptions, agreeing on definitions of excellence, and using rhetoric as a tool to improve spoken language, analytical reading and effective writing across the curriculum

Notes

1 Bernstein, B. (2000) *Pedagogy, symbolic control, and identity,* Rowman & Littlefield Publishers, Lanham, Maryland.

2 Robinson. M. (2013) *Trivium*, Independent Thinking Press, Carmarthen.

3 Wiliam, D. (2013) *Principled Curriculum Design*, SSAT.

4 Hirsch, E.D., Kett, J.F., and Trefil, J.S. (1988) *The dictionary of cultural literacy*. Houghton Mifflin Harcourt, Boston.

5 https://www.theguardian.com/education/2014/nov/25/daisy-christodoulou-seven-myths-education-profile

6 Muller, J. (2014) *'Every picture tells a story: Epistemological access and knowledge', Education as Change,* 18, 2, 255–269, https://doi.org/*10.1080/16823206.2014.932256*

7 Oracy Education Commission. (2024, October). *We Need to Talk: The report of the Commission on the Future of Oracy Education in England.* Retrieved from https://oracyeducationcommission.co.uk/wp-content/uploads/2024/10/Future-of-Oracy-v23-web-13.pdf

8 Oracy Education Commission. (2024) *We Need to Talk: The report of the Commission on the Future of Oracy Education in England.* Retrieved from https://oracyeducationcommission.co.uk/wp-content/uploads/2024/10/Future-of-Oracy-v23-web-13.pdf

9 Ofsted. (2024) *Telling the story: the English education subject report.* Research and analysis. Retrieved from https://www.gov.uk/government/publications/subject-report-series-english/telling-the-story-the-english-education-subject-report

10 Ofsted. (2024) *Telling the story: the English education subject report.* Research and analysis. Retrieved from https://www.gov.uk/government/publications/subject-report-series-english/telling-the-story-the-english-education-subject-report

11 Ofsted. (2024) *Telling the story: the English education subject report.* Research and analysis. Retrieved from https://www.gov.uk/government/publications/subject-report-series-english/telling-the-story-the-english-education-subject-report

12 Counsell, C. (2018) *The indirect manifestation of knowledge: final performance as deceiver and guide.* Available at: https://thedignityofthethingblog.wordpress.com/

13 Robinson, M. (2020) *Organising Knowledge: On Triangles and Ts and Russian Dolls,* Available at: Organising Knowledge: On Triangles and Ts and Russian Dolls. – Trivium 21c Ltd.).

14 These stand for (Direct Address), Alliteration, Facts, Opinions, Rhetorical Questions, Emotive Language, Statistics, Tricolon. For more on this see, Holmes-Henderson, A.

(2025). Not seeing the wood for DAFOREST: rhetoric in the English classroom. English in Education, *59*(4), 298–303. https://doi.org/10.1080/04250494.2025.2563610

15 Hill, C. and Howard, K. (2020) *Symbiosis: The curriculum and the classroom.* John Catt.

16 See Kueh, R. *A Disciplinary Hearing* in Chater, M. (2020) *Reforming RE: Power and Knowledge in a Worldviews Curriculum,* John Catt, Melton.

17 Chan, Fancourt and Guilfoyle (2020) show in a 'quantitative analysis of frequency in thirty-five local authority schools 'although argumentation was never mentioned, other cognates were always present'. They note that 'the importance of developing students' ability to argue effectively is generally recognised... what this means within religious education has not been thoroughly investigated'.

18 Rodriguez-Casado, C. and McMillan, C. (2023) 'Monitoring students' use of disciplinary language in Religious Education' in *RE: ONLINE.* – Available at: https://www.reonline.org.uk/research/monitoring-students-use-of-disciplinary-language-in-religious-education/

6 The implementation of rhetoric in school curriculum design, delivery and continued evaluation

Drawing on the Education Endowment Foundation's (EEF) framework and accompanying guidance for effective implementation in schools (Sharples et al. 2024),[1] this chapter explores the key principles of implementation for those schools keen to get started on introducing the study of rhetoric for their students. Highlighting possible points of fragility, the chapter draws attention to common pitfalls encountered when making changes to curricula, outlines how teachers and leaders might mitigate against these, and supports colleagues with a considered approach to curriculum to introduce and sustain rhetoric as part of their enacted offer for students in the classroom.

What is effective implementation and why does it matter?

Implementation plays a critical role in the development and delivery of a rhetoric framework as an integrated part of a subject or whole-school curriculum; we argue that it is the greatest indicator of success to ensure the substance of any strategy is effectively universally understood and therefore effectively enacted as a living, breathing improvement to what is already in place. As we covered in Chapter 5, 50% of any successful initiative in schools is in the substance of the thing, and the other 50% relies upon meaningful implementation.

Where we feel that we have made a compelling case for the explicit teaching of rhetoric in schools, we are not naive to the work that is needed to develop a curriculum that holds fidelity to some of the principles of rhetoric discussed earlier in this book, or indeed the labour of love that is a never-finished, ever-evolving, living, breathing curriculum. Thinking about implementation ahead of leading any adaptation of system-level or indeed local-level curriculum, whether that be across

DOI: 10.4324/9781003409069-8

a number of schools, one school or even a subject or phase, this practice of planning ahead and considering the anticipated impact(s) of the change before changing anything enables all colleagues to know, understand and apply change in a way that has a shared vision and intention. When applying any changes to curriculum at a national or local level, effective implementation principles help to ensure that the change is planned for, managed and monitored for effectiveness in a way that avoids the notion of what Kahnemann, Sibony and Sunstein refer to as the 'noise' of human judgement.[2] As subject and educational advocates, we often lean into our cognitive biases and perspectives when making decisions, and the curriculum is no exception.

Like any key change to the curriculum, we should practise caution in making assumptions that any one contributing factor will lead to significant change. Curriculum provision and delivery relies not just on the substance of a robust curriculum, but above all else, effective teaching to ensure that delivery is faithful to the intended knowledge encompassed within the initial design, and also the advocacy to the subject being taught so that, as Livingstone stipulates, 'the test of a successful education is not the amount of knowledge that a pupil takes away from school, but his appetite to know and his capacity to learn'.[3] This means that when considering what to teach with regard to rhetoric, we must also consider how to teach it most effectively. This carries implications for individual teachers, of course, but more importantly, how they contribute to the curriculum so that it is greater than the sum of its parts.

Curriculum change is therefore fundamental to its evolution – knowledge does not sit in stasis, after all – and so knowing how to apply the leading principles of implementation ahead of any changes you might make as a result of reading this book will ensure that (a) you are able to monitor the impact of the change effectively, and (b) you are able to support your own professional journey and that of colleagues with delivery once change is underway.

Why do we need to consider implementation alongside rhetoric?

The process of implementation is especially pertinent to incorporating rhetoric into a school curriculum offer, because we know that teaching rhetoric is not yet a commonplace practice in our schools. Given the systemic challenges faced by young people in UK schools regarding the disadvantage gap, literacy levels and a depleting foundational knowledge and understanding around high-quality oracy, we find it odd that rhetoric is somewhat of a luxury feature of the curriculum, typically placed only in English subject curriculum provision, if at all. Yet, we argue fervently that this is an entitlement for all children so that they cannot just navigate the world but rather come to understand the way in which language shapes it. Rhetoric is not yet part of the universal offer for learners, but it indeed should be.

The writing framework released by the Department of Education in 2025 supports the inclusion of rhetoric as part of a progression model, stating, 'the national curriculum requires pupils to draw on knowledge of literary and rhetorical devices from their reading and listening to enhance the impact of their writing'.[4] This explicit link between reading and writing, using knowledge of rhetoric, means that there is scope to clearly define excellence with colleagues ahead of the process of implementation. For many colleagues, this will not have featured as part of their undergraduate study or initial teacher training, where we know subject content knowledge is variable. For many students, primary school study of reading and writing will predominantly focus on building foundational knowledge needed to access curriculum content at a later point. This means that for both teachers and learners in a school, they may never have been inducted into a secure understanding of what rhetoric is, how it shapes written and spoken communication, the ways in which it can shape thought, and how they might set about the process of rhetorical analysis and evaluation.

This makes purposeful implementation a fundamental consideration for rhetoric.

Starting any change process with a strong mental model for the implementation of rhetoric will not only challenge a limited approach but will set colleagues in good stead for being able to clearly name the intended changes, monitor them as part of the process, and evaluate where implementation has been successful. We could not have possibly missed this section out, because it would be like giving you all the food without the recipe.

- Implementation and change management are core components of curriculum
- Teaching rhetoric is essential, but not yet commonplace
- Teachers must therefore be supported during implementation planning
- A strong model for implementation will ensure that the introduction of rhetoric is a success

The EEF guidance report (Sharples et al. 2020) states, 'an "implementation-friendly" climate cannot be created overnight'. Outlining the problem of practice, why it exists, the potential solution and direction of travel can be hugely reassuring for those excited to develop rhetoric as a feature in your school. We will take you through the stages of initial implementation, including the preparatory work and process of sustainability; we would ask of you, reader, that you consider how these can become collective endeavours to bring brilliant colleagues along with you on the journey.

Creating a strong Theory of Change

Teaching rhetoric and integrating it within your curriculum offer might feel like a monumental change, and schools are busy places. There might be competing priorities for time; other curriculum-related initiatives; teaching principles in place that could potentially aid or inhibit some of the considerations, and it is for us as educators to weigh up these as part of effective change management. For school and subject or phase leaders especially, our role is to support colleagues to navigate change as a process of collaboration, because a well-thought-through implementation process will acknowledge potential difficulties and signpost what success looks like. In short? New things are hard, even when they're brilliant, because they're new.

To address this, a Theory of Change (ToC) provides an essential framework for ensuring that interventions are underpinned by clear logic, robust evidence and measurable outcomes. The EEF[5] has emphasised the importance of ToC as a foundation for effective educational interventions, advocating for its use in both the design and evaluation of programmes (Sharples at el. 2020). Before engaging in pre-implementation or implementation, school leaders must first interrogate three fundamental questions alluded to Chapter 5.

What problem are we trying to solve? Why this, why now?

What does good look like, and can we distil this into active ingredients to ensure precision and tangibility? For example, if the curriculum vision is to ensure all children 'be experts in the use of rhetoric', what does that mean? What does it look like? How can it be measured?

Where are the short-term and long-term outcomes so that, in three, six or twelve months, we can hold ourselves accountable using robust data? What data are we collecting, and why robust?

These principles ensure that implementation is not only aspirational but also measurable, evidence-informed and sustainable.

Establishing a clear rationale: why this, why now?

Educational initiatives must begin with a precise articulation of the issue they seek to address, and this will help to direct where you start with introducing rhetoric, in alignment with the evaluation of the current curriculum and quality of existing teaching. Too often, schools adopt interventions based on external pressures, sector trends or anecdotal successes elsewhere, without a rigorous assessment of their relevance to their specific context. A ToC compels leaders to diagnose the root causes of the problem and justify why a particular approach is the most appropriate and timely response.

For rhetoric, this diagnostic phase should include the following aspects:

Contextual analysis: What specific challenges do students face? Are these issues systemic, or are they context-dependent? Is this the cohort-specific issue? What root causes have we considered so that this ToC is not just responsive to the problem at hand but gets upstream on why it was even a problem? For example, if we are seeing a downward trend in the way students interact with fake news, it may be that PSHE can support in implementation through social media use. Or, if the most critical problem is continued underperformance in non-fiction writing in English, then perhaps the problem is systemic and curriculum-focused, and should start with English ahead of later scale-up. Or, perhaps students are demonstrating limited understanding of sources in History or Religious Education when prompted to consider the intentionality of texts or sources in Key Stage 3, where students report low motivation, especially students with SEND, which is leading to a drop in attainment for these students at a later point. Using a range of data, but also in a way that tells a story of both the macro level and the granular, helps us to name the problem of practice that, if attended to, would lead to improvement that could be realistically measured.

Evidence review: What does the research or evidence base offer about effective solutions? Have similar approaches been successful in comparable contexts? Do we know what good looks like? This book might act as a good starting point in employing the case studies shared, but which schools locally may have explored teaching rhetoric and could offer their own successes and learning points? What does this look like in other educational stages? This will enable you or your team to develop a mental model for what change may look like.

Strategic alignment: Does this change align with existing school priorities, your or your team's capacity, and resource availability? Are we inadvertently competing with any other strategic aims, and how could this be channelled as part of implementation planning? For example, reviewing existing writing frameworks across phases or subjects ahead of the construction of something new will ensure such synergy instead of introducing tensions. Equally, the creation of a working party to provide multiple lenses in early implementation will help to eradicate competing processes and practices.

Defining the solution

Once the rationale has been established, the next step is to define what excellence looks like. A common pitfall can sometimes be a reliance on broad, loosely defined objectives, such as 'improving written work' or 'enhancing reading analysis', without clarity on the specific mechanisms that will drive change.

A well-constructed ToC requires schools to first identify active ingredients. What are the non-negotiable components of implementing rhetoric that will drive impact? For example, in a literacy intervention with selected students to start, is it the frequency of exposure to texts, the quality of guided instruction when teachers model and exemplify, or the creation and application of specific frameworks to teach writing using rhetoric that will yield success? This level of specificity is critical for both implementation and evaluation. Without clearly defined active ingredients, the definition of excellence risks becoming fragmented through being open to interpretation, with schools investing considerable effort without a clear understanding of what is driving or hindering progress. For instance, if we define the active ingredient as 'students will feel more confident writing using rhetorical devices', we must consider: which devices? Confident after how much input and practice? How will we measure this in a way that equates confidence with learning? Being specific will enable us to gather the right data to measure in the right way, avoiding tokenism. We need to get under the skin of the student experience in the early stages of implementation.

Short-term and long-term outcomes

A fundamental weakness in implementation is the absence of rigorous impact evaluation. Without clearly defined short-term and long-term outcomes, teachers, teams or schools can sometimes fail to assess whether their efforts are translating into meaningful change. Or other priorities emerge, and the impact-measurement aspect of implementation is lost altogether. This is why curriculum evaluation is highly subjective, and a ToC aims to succinctly capture the milestone points that an individual or team should identify and celebrate.

- **Short-term outcomes:** These should capture early indicators of success, such as changes in teacher practice, pupil engagement or shifts in attitudes and confidence. These are often precursors to more significant improvements in attainment or, indeed, in teacher practice, which may come later as teachers become more confident in their approach.
- **Long-term outcomes:** These should assess whether the changes made are leading to measurable improvements in knowledge, skills or perception of success. There may be quality assurance data from lessons that can support any inferences made. Student attainment data may also show an upward trend.

Crucially, these outcomes are measurable, evidence-informed and subject to rigorous data collection and analysis.

Here is how a ToC might look as a starting framework:

Define the problem	Lay out the solution and active ingredients of this solution	Explain the inputs (for teachers and students)	Capture the short-term outcome (one to two terms)	Clarify the long-term outcome (one year)	Specify how you will know there has been a positive impact

And so for a teacher or team constructing a ToC for any curriculum alteration, or in this case, introducing the study of rhetoric, it may look like this:

Define the problem	Lay out the solution and active ingredients of this solution	Explain the inputs	Capture the short-term outcome	Clarify the long-term outcome	Specify how you will know there has been a positive impact
Children are unable to write high-quality non-fiction texts	All children are able to write a series of non-fiction texts of varying forms with fluency	Teacher development in English and History regarding rhetoric as a framework for non-fiction, and refresh of modelling in the classroom. English to lead this component with both teams	Students will write three types of non-fiction in Year 7	Student performance in Year 7 non-fiction units will improve	Assessment data
		Student and parent input regarding the teaching of rhetoric in KS3	All students will analyse exemplars, where writing will be prefaced with analysis of a high-quality model	Students will be able to identify appeals to ethos, logos and pathos in Year 8 for future learning	Subject lead feedback through Quality Assurance
		Co-creation of an interleaved sequence using high-quality exemplars and shared language and framework for reading and writing using rhetoric	All students will know ethos, logos and pathos and apply this to their written work	Teachers will feel a strong sense of confidence in delivering this aspect of rhetoric study	Lesson observations and teacher perception data

The EEF recommends embedding evaluation mechanisms from the outset of implementation, ensuring that data collection aligns with the programme's causal assumptions and therefore provides actionable insights (Sharples et al. 2024). Moreover, this process enables schools to (a) distinguish between a theory failure, (b) whether there was another area of the taught curriculum or another cohort where implementing change may have been more effective or easier to define; or implementation failure, (c) where the colleagues driving the change did not have a shared definition of excellence or (d) professional development was not provided to ensure knowledge building and sharing was available for teachers.

The urgency of school improvement must not come at the expense of strategic rigour, and good implementation plans mitigate against speed without intention. Without a well-defined ToC, schools risk investing time and resources in initiatives that are fragmented, poorly executed and subsequently, difficult to evaluate.

The question for anyone looking to get started is not simply what to implement, but why, how and with what evidence? Those who engage with these questions systematically will be best placed to drive transformational change. The EEF (Sharples et al. 2024) highlights that the most effective initiatives are those that begin with clarity of purpose, precision in execution and accountability in evaluation. A ToC provides leaders and teachers with a framework to navigate this complexity, ensuring that every decision is intentional, every strategy is well-defined and every outcome is measurable.

As leaders supporting colleagues with this work, your role is not just to implement change but to lead it with rigour and thoughtfulness. The schools that consistently improve are not those that do the most but those that do the right things, in the right way, at the right time.

- Where is an absence of teaching rhetoric having a detrimental impact on young people's attainment or experience? What is my dataset to support this?
- What specific outcomes am I aiming to achieve in the next 3, 6 and 12 months? How will I measure success?
- Have I clearly identified the active ingredients of my chosen approach? What are the risks of mutation, dilution or inconsistency? What might the common misconceptions be about rhetoric? Who will be our experts?

What does strong implementation look like?

Once you have formed a ToC, it is worth sharing with colleagues to stress-test the language and clarity. Now it is time to think about how to bring it to fruition.

In 2024, the EEF republished its guidance for implementation in schools,[6] and the modifications made are a welcome addition to this part of the book. Whilst there are several well-substantiated models that provide a framework for effective implementation, the EEF's updated guidance is most relevant to any teacher or leader working in schools currently: the guidance is well-positioned to understand the important role that collective efficacy and readiness for change play in the busy environment of schools. It provides a roadmap for ascertaining these key aspects ahead of implementation.

Here, we will look at each stage of the model in turn and then explore how this framework would apply to a colleague or team of colleagues seeking to integrate rhetoric as part of their curriculum, particularly in consideration of the different phases and contexts.

Exploring the foundations of implementation

Successful implementation in schools does not happen by accident. It requires a deliberate and structured process, ensuring that changes are evidence-informed, feasible and suited to the school's context. The first stage of this process, ***Explore***, is crucial in laying the groundwork for effective implementation. Schools must resist the temptation to rush into adopting new initiatives without first diagnosing the problem they seek to address (which we've done). This means engaging in a systematic review of existing practices, assessing pupil needs and considering the barriers and enablers that will influence the implementation process. Too often, initiatives fail not because they are ineffective but because they are poorly matched to the school's specific challenges and strengths.

There is also value in finding out what's working elsewhere and gathering insights into what teaching rhetoric looks like in other contexts. When writing this book, we sampled the curriculum overviews of 100 schools (80 primary, 20 secondary, all state schools), and 72 schools made explicit reference to rhetoric as part of their curriculum offer. This is exciting! It means we are building and sharing knowledge and are able to learn from each other to better understand what this looks like in practice.

Finally, in this early stage, engaging a range of stakeholders – including teachers, pupils and parents – helps in identifying potential challenges early and generating collective buy-in, especially where schools may want to raise debate and discussion around more sensitive but socially relevant issues. By establishing a shared understanding of the problem and possible solutions, schools can move into the next stage with confidence that they are pursuing teaching rhetoric in a way that has genuine potential to improve outcomes.

- Collate research to support the introduction of rhetoric and support the rationale for why

- Learn from other settings regarding their journey of implementation
- Engage with key stakeholders to gain their insights or questions

Preparing for effective implementation

Once a school or team of colleagues sets out an intention to teach rhetoric, the focus shifts to preparation. The ***Prepare*** phase is where clarity, coherence and capacity-building take centre stage. This stage requires us to develop a clear implementation plan, ensuring that staff understand not only what will change but also why the change is necessary. As part of this, it is essential to define the active ingredients from the ToC, specifying what 'good' implementation looks like, and a monitoring framework that will allow for experimentation before we might see long-term change in the classroom.

For instance, this might mean making time for subject knowledge development for teachers from a leading expert, or the collaborative collation of materials so teachers can collectively consider: which texts? Why? Or, what sequence to teach the employment of rhetorical devices and through which examples? Why? These subject-specific debates are deeply fulfilling to teachers when change is imminent.[7]

Preparation also involves building the necessary conditions for success. This means securing leadership support and ensuring teachers involved have access to high-quality professional development and the opportunity to see each other's practice as they trial their approaches. There is nothing more galvanising in the early stages of trialling rhetoric than watching colleagues bring the curriculum to life, and then be able to share reflections, capture successes and collectively make adaptations. Dedicating time that will be used to get out of the classroom ahead of delivery will provide healthy accountability for when school life gets rather hectic further down the line, and there is a potential for other priorities to steal such time.

- Ensure time is dedicated ahead of delivery for teachers to learn from one another
- Keep the model of excellence at the forefront of plans for delivery
- Cultivate a culture of watching and learning from other teachers

Delivery

With a strong foundation in place, the ***Deliver*** stage marks the transition from planning to action. This phase is often the most challenging, as it requires teachers to navigate the complexities of curriculum enactment and to be able to not only manage their cognitive load with newer, less familiar content in the classroom, but to be able to evaluate delivery following a lesson or sequence of lessons.

Implementation is rarely a linear process; setbacks are inevitable, and we should be prepared to adapt our approach based on emerging insights over time. The key to success at this stage is treating implementation as a continual journey rather than a fixed plan: we are guided by theories of change as our shared ambition for teaching rhetoric, but the way in which we reach that ambition? It is collectively acknowledged that this will have flexibility to ensure we don't sink time and energy into less effective approaches.

Effective delivery hinges on ongoing support and monitoring. We should provide timely reminders and prompts to reinforce key messages and sustain momentum if teachers or teams are driving this piece of work, ensuring it remains a priority. Professional development should not exist as a one-off event but should continue throughout the implementation period, incorporating opportunities for staff to reflect, share experiences and refine their practice. It might be that a teacher narrates their planning for the week ahead, reflecting on lessons learned from the previous sequence of teaching; or perhaps, the team hears from another school where they are slightly further along in implementation, and can share how they refined their writing framework from its initial draft through a series of iterations as a result of putting it to use in the classroom. Leadership of this integration within the curriculum plays a crucial role here, not only in modelling commitment to the initiative but also in creating an environment where staff feel supported in making incremental improvements.

In the delivery stage, there is much merit in taking stock of the successes and change fatigue of teachers driving this work: teaching new content can feel intimidating, and it will be important to make space for exemplification but also hearing the collective challenges. If colleagues are trying to create models live in the classroom, how can collective time be spent co-constructing these? If one colleague has had a brilliantly positive experience of annotating a speech during teaching, could they pre-record this so the rest of the cohort can benefit? Perhaps a teacher is highly confident in articulating the framework of rhetoric and has subsequently designed retrieval practice questions to ensure this is checked ahead of the next stage of students' learning. The opportunities for collaboration and repurposing the hard efforts of teachers are endless at this stage and must be leveraged accordingly.

Finally, data collection will be a valuable part of the process, allowing for adjustments in response to challenges. Sampling students' feelings of success, teachers' experiences during enactment and the connections they see students might make in later learning will all be beneficial learning reflections. Teachers should be proactive in identifying and addressing implementation barriers as they arise, leveraging the expertise of other staff who have successfully adopted the approach to support others. By viewing implementation as an iterative process rather than a one-off event, schools can increase the likelihood of long-term success.

- Treat a certain degree of 'false failure' as inevitable when implementing new and therefore less familiar content

- Provide continued opportunities for learning and collaboration, especially to reduce the cognitive load of teachers
- View delivery, monitoring and refinement as an iterative process

Sustaining change

Sustaining implementation is perhaps the most overlooked stage of the process. Too often, we invest significant effort in launching an initiative only for it to fade away over time. Curriculum changes are made, and we deny ourselves the process of taking stock of the improvements seen as a result. We need to reflect on the impacts of staff turnover, when the ambition and rationale for these changes is lost and all that remains is the curriculum plan without the narrative of the journey.

Introducing rhetoric as part of a taught curriculum needs sustaining, so that shared definitions of what good looks like continue to receive the collective wisdom of teachers, and so that enactment in the classroom continues to be a brilliant experience for young people. There is also a point of note here regarding the real-world interaction of teaching rhetoric, and the importance for teachers to review stimulus content in a way that aligns with the world that pupils experience. For example, as we finish up this chapter, Charlie Kirk was shot at a rally in America, and a plethora of his speeches and debates have resurfaced and flooded social media in his memory. Equally, riots continue in England concerning immigration, with key politicians addressing the press. We have a social responsibility to review what we use to teach children the criticality of current affairs, to make an informed opinion of social and civic matters. Rhetoric is a crucial vehicle for doing that: it speaks to the social and historical, but most importantly, to understanding the human condition in an age of AI.

A common pitfall at this stage is assuming that once an intervention has been introduced, it will continue indefinitely without further effort. In reality, schools must actively work to maintain implementation fidelity. This means reinforcing key messages, ensuring new staff in a subject team receive appropriate training, or perhaps integrating successful components of the experience into broader school structures, or as part of a wider approach to provide students with the opportunity to learn how language can be used for manipulative purposes. It may simply be by extending the offer through to other cohorts, or by employing some of the approaches to another key stage when approaching writing, reading or speaking. A consideration here is the roast chicken analogy, to avoid lethal mutations as part of a scale-up process: children must see a roast chicken in order to cook one. Put all the more simply, scale-up should ensure that students continue to see high-quality examples. They need to see multiple models of what excellence can look like.

Additionally, schools should periodically review their implementation efforts, assessing whether the approach continues to meet pupil needs. They should make evidence-informed decisions about sustaining, scaling or adapting the approach. Returning to the ToC for those all-important indicators of the data we believed would most effectively ascertain success will help to determine what might come next.

By following a structured yet flexible implementation process – moving through the Explore, Prepare, Deliver and Sustain stages – schools can maximise the impact of their initiatives. The key takeaway is that implementation is not a singular event but an ongoing process of learning, adaptation and improvement. With careful planning, strong leadership and a commitment to continuous refinement, schools can create meaningful and lasting change in their classrooms.

- Review stimulus texts, teaching materials and frameworks collectively to ensure they are ambitious, relevant, and teachers are confident to teach them with authenticity
- Consider what scale-up looks like and why that appears to be the most prominent priority next
- Remember principles of learning in scale-up, such as examples ahead of student application, succinct teacher instruction or retrieving relevant prior knowledge

Evaluating a rhetoric curriculum

Implementing a rhetoric curriculum is just the beginning of the journey; ensuring its effectiveness over time requires rigorous evaluation, reflection and refinement. This means that you, or your team should consider how to evaluate quality over time, but also some of the mechanisms that we have used over the years in schools and Trusts to support with this process. We will now explore how to evaluate a rhetoric curriculum once it has been implemented, using a combination of collaborative planning, subject-specific professional development, and wider quality assurance mechanisms.

Establishing clear success criteria

To return to our exploration into curriculum, evaluation must begin with clarity about what success looks like. Schools need to define the knowledge, skills and attitudes that students should develop through their rhetoric curriculum. These might include high-quality oracy, structured thinking, persuasive writing and critical engagement with texts. Success criteria should be developed collaboratively, with input from teachers, students and school leaders. By aligning evaluation metrics with these objectives, schools can ensure that assessment mechanisms reflect meaningful learning rather than superficial engagement.

What data do we have at our disposal, and does this give us an indication of quality. Here are some perspectives that will be useful when constructing your own rationale for data-driven improvement as an iterative process.

The educational landscape is replete with potential sources of noise that can distort our perception of what constitutes improvement and effectiveness. Here are some key examples:

Confirmation bias: We tend to favour information that confirms our existing beliefs and we downplay evidence that contradicts them. As a result, we lean towards presenting information or delivery of initiatives in a way that suits our beliefs and values. This might mean that we think rhetoric is a brilliant offer for young people and so are encouraging others to adopt an approach because it's the choice we are most comfortable with, or looking at data through a singular lens and drawing conclusions rather than posing questions. This is especially pertinent when taking snapshots of data from the everyday movement and operation of schools, and equally, those closest may sometimes have distorted perceptions of the current state of play. This can lead to a selective evaluation of data and a reluctance to consider alternative approaches to school improvement.

The availability heuristic: We judge the likelihood of an event based on the ease with which examples come to mind. This can lead to overestimating the prevalence of certain limitations and neglecting others. For example, 'Year Nine are awful at this' may be the conclusion that Kat drew in her ITT year, as a result of teaching Year Nine for approximately twelve hours of their entire secondary school education. Equally, 'this dip in attainment means rhetoric has made attainment worse' without looking at data through different lenses or looking at an aspect of school using one dataset to draw a comprehensive judgement will lead to a reliance on leaning towards what we think we know to be true, and leaning away from what we think we know to not be as such. Taking a balanced and cautious approach to data analysis and drawing on multiple bodies of evidence, such as student voice, teaching quality, and attainment data will mitigate against this.

The halo effect: A positive impression of one aspect of a school (e.g., curriculum) can lead to an overly positive evaluation of other aspects (e.g., teaching quality). This can hinder the identification of areas that require further evaluation. For example, if our impression of the quality of the curriculum is that it is good, so we might see the enacted curriculum as equally good in the process. This may also translate into poor proxies for learning; we may see a quiet classroom and assign learning to that environment because children are quiet and busy. This is why, when evaluating curriculum enactment in classrooms, it's helpful to go in pairs and stress-test one another's biases, but also to hold one another to account. Defining a concept of quality is a good way to mitigate against misconceptions that what we see means it is more amazing than reality dictates and keeps our 'noise' in check.

Curating meaningful evaluation of rhetoric study in your school

Fortunately, just having an awareness of the strengths and limitations of collating different data helps here. However, there is a range of ways that this might take shape through the lens of schools and the practice of school and system leaders:

Use multiple sets of data: We always recommend using three sets of data to draw inferences – whether that be attainment data, teacher or student voice or observed typicality in the classroom. Employing this multi-pronged approach can provide a more holistic understanding of school performance.

Engage in regular collaboration: Teachers can develop their ability to make sound judgements by engaging in deliberate practice. Ensuring that implementation and scale-up activities, especially around less familiar content, don't fall to just one person reduces bias in our ongoing evaluation processes.

Normalise error: Irrespective of professional development or opportunities to collaborate, in the early stages of trialling, things will fail in the classroom. Such is the inevitability of trialling new content with children who are unlikely to have any relevant prior knowledge. Teachers and teams can design developmental discussions using the approach of 'this "appears" to be working well, but let's take a closer look, so we can decide what's next'. Celebrating milestones with professional curiosity and scepticism, before co-constructing next steps around what's not quite working, will lead to fewer colleagues feeling like they're not quite getting it right. We can collectively work on the challenges encountered.

The role of collaborative planning in evaluation

Collaborative planning should remain central even after implementation, ensuring that curriculum evaluation is a shared endeavour rather than an isolated exercise. Regular departmental discussions, co-planning sessions and reflective practice meetings help maintain coherence and allow teachers to assess how the curriculum is being embedded across different contexts.

A key approach is to use professional learning communities (PLCs) to review student progress, share teaching strategies and refine curriculum delivery. For rhetoric, this might involve teachers bringing examples of student speeches, essays and discussions to examine patterns in student understanding and areas that require greater emphasis. It might be that student work is used to gauge where common misconceptions or knowledge gaps are forming, and this can then used to refine teaching materials. Collaboration in implementation will ensure problems are addressed together.

Other helpful ways to evaluate as a collective group

Robust quality assurance mechanisms ensure that the rhetoric curriculum maintains the initial ambition of your ToC. Teachers can explore different ways to evaluate success in a range of ways as scale-up continues or implementation is further refined.

Curriculum mapping as a team can help to interrogate where other areas of the curriculum would benefit the introduction of, or return to, rhetoric study, thinking about the intention of that stage in the curriculum model. Assessment moderation is also a useful activity for the team to see how students are grappling with content, but also to repurpose student work in taught materials for future use. Finally, a consideration of the way in which the enrichment offer enables young people to explore what is being taught in a way that enables them a pursuit of knowledge outside of the classroom is another interesting evaluation. For example, is there a debating club in session? What is the correlation between those students who attend it and their attainment in rhetoric-related components of the curriculum?

These mechanisms should not operate in isolation but feed into a cycle of continuous improvement, where findings are used to inform professional development, resource allocation and curriculum refinement.

An infrastructure that encourages continual professional curiosity

A well-evaluated rhetoric curriculum should lead to sustainable, long-term improvements in teaching and learning. Schools should regularly revisit their evaluation strategies, ensuring they evolve alongside emerging research, but are sensitive to subject-specific nuances. Establishing a culture of critical reflection, where teachers can feel empowered to question and refine their approach to integrating rhetoric, ensures that rhetoric remains a living, breathing component of school life rather than merely a static curriculum document.

- Evaluation is a process of triangulating data that tells potentially differing stories
- Colleagues can work collaboratively to stress test one another's theories or inferences and to reduce biases
- Evaluation should be a process of enquiry, refinement and continual review so that the offer incrementally improves over time

A note on interdisciplinary integration of rhetoric

Once rhetoric has been embedded in one subject, it might be that exploring its interdisciplinary application enhances its impact. Subjects and phases can take several approaches to achieve this as part of the scale-up phase of implementation, and we would urge caution in doing so before that point or at least have specific parameters for an approach that spans multiple subjects in earlier stages. The reasons are two-fold: first of all, it makes it more difficult to support colleagues in establishing a shared language and approach, and therefore more difficult to ascertain success through an increased likelihood of mutations in the enacted curriculum. The second point recalls the caution of distorting subject specialisms, and to do so only where it is mutually beneficial to subjects. Put simply, what works for science will not work for Geography, and so on, and so forth. Enabling subject experts to highlight where it would be helpful to explore interdisciplinary strategies that will not tamper with the procedures of the subject is the most accurate indicator here.

Yet, there are certain aspects that teams and schools may wish to explore. One such method is adopting universal debate and discussion techniques across subjects, ensuring students consistently refine their ability to identify rhetoric in great works and apply this knowledge to the construction of their own spoken debates. For example, History lessons could use structured debates on historical interpretations, while Science classes could engage students in ethical discussions about emerging scientific developments.

Another approach is applying *ethos*, *logos*, and *pathos* in a context-specific manner across subjects. In English, students might analyse how novelists employ rhetorical appeals to influence readers, whereas in Geography, they might explore how climate activists use rhetoric to shape public opinion. By tailoring rhetorical concepts to each subject's unique demands, students gain a deeper, more concrete understanding of persuasive communication.

Again, collaborative planning between departments can also highlight opportunities to integrate rhetoric into subject curricula. Teachers from different disciplines can identify overlapping areas where rhetorical skills enhance learning. For instance, Philosophy and Politics teachers might work together to develop a unit on argument construction, helping students evaluate bias and logical fallacies.

Additionally, the PSHE and Citizenship curriculum presents a valuable opportunity to explore rhetoric's societal implications. Teaching students about rhetoric in conspiracy theories, social media manipulation and the portrayal of misogyny in news coverage equips them with critical literacy skills essential for navigating modern media landscapes. Revisiting rhetorical strategies within PSHE ensures students see rhetoric not just as an academic skill but as a crucial tool for understanding and responding to the world around them.

By embedding rhetoric across multiple subjects, schools can reinforce its value as a vital life skill, equipping students to analyse, engage with and challenge the arguments they encounter in diverse contexts. An interdisciplinary approach ensures that rhetoric becomes a cohesive part of a student's educational experience, fostering articulate, critical thinkers who can navigate complex ideas with confidence. We want citizens who can listen attentively to others, who can reach consensus and who can protest effectively. Future productive civic dialogue requires these skills.

The role of de-implementation in curriculum evolution

And finally, this brings us to the important role that de-implementation holds here when attempting to successfully implement a rhetoric curriculum. It is vital to review existing mechanisms, materials and approaches and determine honestly and professionally, whether they are still fit for purpose. De-implementation is not about undoing progress but about refining and repurposing structures to best serve the school's evolving needs.

One of the most significant barriers to meaningful curriculum development is time, or rather, the lack of it. If teachers are expected to integrate rhetoric into their subject areas, they need protected time for curriculum development. Meetings should shift to a continued focus on collaborative curriculum planning. Prioritising curriculum design within meeting structures ensures that implementation is deliberate and high-quality. Most importantly, it enables a platform for those teachers who are finding success in the earlier stages of implementation to share this knowledge with others.

Additionally, teachers need time to explore and document models of excellence in rhetoric teaching, task design, modelling and independent practice before they begin creating materials for students. Without this, there is a risk that rhetoric is implemented inconsistently across subjects. Schools should provide opportunities for educators to engage with exemplary practice, either through observation, video analysis or discussion with expert colleagues. This ensures a shared understanding of best practice before teachers begin adapting materials for their classrooms. Equally, teachers will benefit from sharing models to use retrospectively in feedback lessons with students, to demystify the construction of writing and share clear success criteria for high-quality application of rhetorical devices.

Furthermore, de-implementation provides an opportunity for broader curriculum review. Schools should take this as a chance to reconsider outdated or less effective areas of the curriculum. Where certain content no longer serves students' needs, replacing it with rhetoric-focused learning may enhance engagement and curricular relevance. Questions such as 'Does this area of study still serve its intended purpose?' or 'Would time be better spent strengthening students' rhetorical competence before this written task?' encourage meaningful reflection and ensure that curriculum decisions are intentional.

Finally, embedding de-implementation into evaluation ensures that curriculum improvements are sustainable. Teams should establish review cycles where teachers can reflect on whether they feel confident in delivery, and whether students are making progress, so that they might become experts in rhetoric over time. By continuously assessing and refining their approach, schools can ensure that their rhetoric curriculum remains ambitious, full of challenge and beneficial to students' long-term academic and personal growth, but in a way that is sensitive to teacher workload and classroom practice. Saying 'this isn't quite working' out loud should be an essential competence in building our professional vocabulary.

In summary:

- **Effective implementation is essential** for integrating rhetoric into the curriculum, ensuring that both the substance of the curriculum and the process of enactment are equally robust and well understood by staff.
- **A clear ToC** provides the foundation for the successful introduction of rhetoric, helping schools diagnose the problem, define excellence through active ingredients and establish measurable short- and long-term outcomes.
- **Rhetoric is not yet a universal entitlement,** making purposeful planning vital for teacher subject knowledge, shared frameworks, professional development and building a coherent, evidence-informed rationale for 'why this, why now'
- **The EEF implementation cycle of Explore, Prepare, Deliver, Sustain** offers a structured framework that enables schools to build readiness, plan collaboratively, support colleagues through enactment and refine practice iteratively over time.
- **Sustaining change requires ongoing review,** protection against dilution or mutation, structured induction for new staff and alignment with real-world contexts so that rhetoric remains a meaningful, high-quality and socially relevant component of students' learning.

Notes

1 Sharples, J., Eaton, J. and Boughelaf, J. (2024) *A school's guide to implementation*. Guidance Report. *Education Endowment Foundation.*

2 Kahneman, D., Rosenfield, A.M., Gandhi, L. and Blaser, T. (2016) 'Noise: How to overcome the high, hidden cost of inconsistent decision making', *Harvard Business Review*, 94, 10, 38–46.

3 Sir Richard Livingstone, President of Corpus Christi College, Oxford, address in 1941.

4 Department for Education. (2025) *The writing framework*. GOV.UK. https://assets.publishing.service.gov.uk/media/68bec95444fd43581bda1c86/The_writing_framework_092025.pdf

5 Sharples, J., Albers, B., and Fraser, S. (2020) *Putting evidence to work: A school's guide to implementation*. Education Endowment Foundation. https://dera.ioe.ac.uk/id/eprint/31088/1/EEF-Implementation-Guidance-Report.pdf

6 Sharples, J., Albers, B., and Fraser, S. (2018) *Putting evidence to work: A school's guide to implementation*. Guidance Report. Education Endowment Foundation.
7 Kat has written extensively about the value of subject development time for teachers, most prominently and practically here: https://saysmiss.wordpress.com/2025/05/14/subject-development-time-a-framework-to-support-teacher-development/ and here: https://saysmiss.wordpress.com/2025/05/21/subject-development-time-page-to-practice/

7 Seven principles for teachers and leaders

Final reflections: next steps for school leaders and teachers, and what lies ahead for curriculum

In this book, we have tried to present the historical and social value and relevance of rhetoric, and its alignment with many priorities of the modern classroom teacher. It is important that we consider the origin and history of rhetoric before, considering the way in which the world around children is evolving, and how we have a responsibility to support them. As an older generation curating curriculum, we have a responsibility to help young people cultivate essential skills to thrive in civic life beyond school.

In our set of proposals for how this could be implemented, we have not been naive about the role of school leaders in creating the climate that enables teachers to bring such conceptual thinking to life: if a leader's attention is directed to making something happen, this acts as a key lever that galvanises implementation.

Seven principles for teachers and leaders

1. Rhetoric acts as a vehicle for strong critical engagement with the written and spoken word

At its core, rhetoric concerns persuasion. This ancient framework can help people of all ages to construct and articulate their own position on diverse topics. Deconstructing the communication of others, though, becomes a rhetorical superpower. How is language being used to emotionally manipulate the audience's feelings about the speaker and/or their message? Knowledge of rhetoric helps listeners to become active, not passive, when interrogating the veracity and import of communications. This interrogation extends to delivery; how are gestures, body language, eye contact and vocal variation being used to persuade? Rhetoric gives learners (and teachers!) the skills to read between the lines, separating fact from fiction as critical consumers.

DOI: 10.4324/9781003409069-9

2. Rhetoric has a social and civic function as well as an academic one

In the ancient world, the ability to speak well was an integral element of being a citizen. It was impossible to fulfil the duties of citizenship without rhetorical skills. These were essential for success in the political, religious, mercantile and legal ecosystems. Rhetoric wasn't about 'showing off', it was about productive dialogue in public. By sharing individual perspectives, opinions and arguments, a community could move from conflict to consensus. Education today should not focus on filling the minds of young people with only knowledge and facts. Instead, it should support young people to cultivate the skills which are useful across and beyond the curriculum. In preparing the citizens of the future to make key decisions concerning climate change, geopolitical unrest and food scarcity, we give them, through rhetoric, the skills to use their voices effectively while listening critically to others. Rhetoric acts as a communicative bridge from self-empowerment to civic flourishing.

3. Rhetoric acts as a function to enhance subject teaching, though not at the cost of the subject

It is key to note that the very value of rhetoric, as with all knowledge and experience in our schools, is not designed to act as an isolated intervention, but a thread through which students acquire knowledge, skills and understanding in their pursuit of becoming experts in their own right. This is only possible if we to view rhetoric as a domain, of course, but also as a vehicle through which students see an embellishment of the world around them. Language shifts from words on a page or spoken out loud, to holding a transformative quality for young people. They begin to notice the influential nature of language, deliberate (and less intentional) employment of words and syntax that prompts an audience to be moved emotionally, or even to action.

Teachers and leaders should therefore consider the value that rhetoric holds as part of the taught curriculum, and how this is communicated and revisited with all key stakeholders. We know that the word 'rhetoric' carries a somewhat different and distinctive meaning in its social use in contrast to its educational definition, and so working in partnership with young people and parents to establish the study of rhetoric as a demystifier of language is a core component of implementation. Ensuring that knowing rhetoric is a means to understanding and not distorting language may be a helpful way of framing this, but ultimately, there is a necessity to its place in classroom teaching. If introduced in a meaningful way, students, parents and other key stakeholders will be curious to know more.

4. Be clear in your vision for rhetoric and what it sets out to achieve

As Part A of the book seeks to assert, rhetoric is far from a fad, and whilst it may have only recently re-emerged in conversations about the modern curriculum, it sits at the very heart of ancient teachings that can inform and improve our classrooms today. Yet, it is critical that leaders and teachers seek to interrogate how the purpose and intention of the wider curriculum are nourished further by this addition.

As with any school initiative, being clear in the vision and ambition helps all key stakeholders to see their role in that realisation. It also helps to drive positive and professional behaviours.

Spending time asking these questions has multiple benefits: first of all, colleagues can collectively agree on a shared vision and intention for teaching rhetoric. This builds a shared concept of quality. When all parties are clear in the rationale and the expected outcome, they can hold each other mutually accountable.

5. Strong implementation that has collaboration at the heart

Implementation is a continuous process, and leaders should consider the induction of new staff, continuous professional learning and how quality will be evaluated. What will be the milestones indicating success, when introducing and indeed maintaining rhetoric as part of the taught curriculum? Where schools can showcase the successes, particularly in the early stages of implementation, this helps build collegiality towards a common goal.

The very best implementation planning comes as a result of collaborative thinking at all levels of a staff workforce, and clarity in the goal itself. School leaders should consider the mechanism they will create to capture excellence over time, alongside strong methods of communication to share it at the subject and school levels, as well as with key stakeholders. Finally, there should be a pragmatism to implementation to ensure it will be sustainably sound: taking a 'test and learn' approach, learning from subjects already comfortable with rhetorical frameworks. The humanities, for example, could take lead, supporting a long-term vision in a way that doesn't feel daunting to staff, and supports all staff to see what can be achieved though high quality exemplification shared by peers.

6. A distilled outline of the knowledge, skills and understanding

To avoid capturing this experience as a series of suggested activities, there should be a clear outline of what students will learn, what the sequence of this will be, and how they will practise and apply this knowledge to develop mastery over time. When considering the role of rhetoric as part of the taught curriculum, phase and subject leaders may be prompted to revisit key documents and materials that they already use to enact the curriculum and consider the areas of strength and fragility in how these documents communicate the intention of the designed curriculum. Clarity in what students will know, apply and learn over time, as a result, will act as the anchor language through which leaders can ascertain impact.

Relevant to all curriculum-related work, the role that professional development plays here should be front and centre when considering what will be learned by students and how such an ambition can be realised by teachers. This depends on the training and development they receive as part of planning. If teachers are provided with dedicated time to think about or discuss teaching with peers, they will thrive. Any school strategy that misses out on this vital component will, in our opinion, flounder. Ultimately, strong curriculum enactment comes as a result of depth of thought and collaborative endeavour within teams in bringing it to life effectively.

7. Working with all key stakeholders to make it possible

When all parties invested in the education of children come together around a shared sense of purpose, this is when implementation is truly strengthened. Therefore, it is worth stating that 'with great power comes great responsibility' and this has never been truer than unpacking language in the complexities and polarisation of the modern world. Integrating rhetoric into the curriculum brings responsibilities for teachers regarding exemplification and application. A far cry from writing letters to the Headteacher, persuading them to ditch homework policy, the online world navigated by our children is a universe away from our own childhoods or current algorithmic experience. Instead, recognising the interdependence that rhetoric holds with the lived experience of children, and handling this with critical caution, will support teachers, leaders and other stakeholders in navigating a young person's world with them and supporting them accordingly.

External organisations

There are several organisations already thinking carefully about how they can support this work in schools. We have included a list of associations and organisations that can support school leaders and teachers with much of this thinking ahead of implementation in their own context.

Advocating Classics Education

Association for Citizenship Teaching

Classical Association

Debate Mate

English Association

English and Media Centre

English Speaking Union

Litdrive

National Association for the Teaching of English

TeamEnglish

Voice 21

Further reading

Cooper, Y. (2020) *She Speaks: Speeches that Changed the World from Pankhurst to Greta*, Atlantic Books, London.

Doza, G. (2022) *How to Apologise for Killing a: Rhetoric and the Art of Persuasion*, Canbury Press, Kingston-upon-Thames.

Forsyth, M. (2016) *The Elements of Eloquence: How to Turn the Perfect English Phrase*, Icon Books, London.

Gardner, M. (2026) *Voices of Opportunity: Oracy for social mobility in education*, Routledge, London.

Gaunt, A. and Stott, A. (2019) *Transform Teaching and Learning through Talk: The Oracy Imperative*, R&L Books, London.

Hall, E. (2019) *Aristotle's Way: Ten Ways Ancient Wisdom Can Change Your Life*, Vintage Books, London.

Hasan, M. (2024) *Win Every Argument: The Art of Debating, Persuading and Public Speaking*, Macmillan Press, London.

Heinrichs, J. (2010) *Winning Arguments: From Aristotle to Obama - Everything You Need to Know About the Art of Persuasion*, Penguin, London.

Lancaster, S. (2022) *Connect! How to Inspire, Influence and Energise Anyone, Anywhere, Anytime*, Heligo Books, London.

Leith, S. (2012) *You Talking to Me? Rhetoric from Aristotle to Obama,* Profile Books, London.

Russell, A. (2021) *Great Women's Speeches: Empowering Voices that Engage and Inspire*, White Lion Books, London.

Szuplat, T. (2024) *Say It Well: Find Your Voice, Speak Your Mind, Inspire Any Audience*, Harper Books, New York.

Toye, R. (2013) *Rhetoric: A very short introduction*, Oxford University Press, Oxford.

Webster, L. (2023) *EMC Approaches to Rhetoric: A Practical Guide for 11-14 year-olds*, English and Media Centre, London.

Wright, T. (2025) *Oracy: The politics of speech education*, Cambridge University Press, Cambridge.

Websites, radio programmes and podcasts

Myblackhistory.net

Americanradioworks.publicradio.org

Almeida Figures of Speech website: https://www.speech.almeida.co.uk/

BBC Radio 4 – The Long History of Argument

Find out more about global rhetorics

Global rhetorics look beyond Greek and Roman conceptions of rhetoric to encompass multi-cultural communicative frameworks. The following resources may be of interest:

https://globalrhetorics.com/ A podcast series, in which global rhetoricians are interviewed.

https://ashr.org/teaching-resources/teaching-history-of-rhetoric/ The links on this site may be particularly useful

Lloyd, K. (2020) *The Routledge Handbook of Comparative World Rhetorics* compares rhetoric across cultures, Routledge, New York.

Afterword: Mary Myatt

The journey through *Reviving Rhetoric* reminds us of something both simple and significant: young people are deeply capable, and they deserve access to the traditions that help them to think well.

Rhetoric is one of those traditions. It has been with us for thousands of years, yet its value feels particularly sharp in these uncertain times. What Arlene and Kat show in this book is that rhetoric is not an optional add-on but a central part of an intellectually serious curriculum.

They invite us to consider rhetoric not only through its classical roots with Plato, Aristotle and the enduring appeals of *ethos*, *logos* and *pathos*, but also through its modern application. They illustrate how rhetoric helps pupils read with discernment, listen with attention and speak with integrity. These are not skills that sit at the edge of education; they are part of helping young people become thoughtful contributors to their communities. In an age of misinformation and digital noise, this work matters.

What is refreshing about *Reviving Rhetoric* is the balance of scholarship and practicality. Arlene and Kat offer clear reasoning for why rhetoric belongs in our schools, and it also sets out what this might look like in practice.

The proposed framework, underpinned by a transparent Theory of Change, encourages us to treat rhetoric as a coherent body of knowledge. We are urged to treat it as something that strengthens learning across the curriculum rather than sitting in isolation. The guidance on design, implementation and evaluation provides helpful guardrails without being prescriptive.

Rhetoric enables young people to make sense of the world and to take part in it with confidence. It gives them the tools to form high-quality arguments and to evaluate the arguments presented to them. This is intellectual work, certainly, but it is also civic work. And when we offer it thoughtfully, as shown in the case studies, young people rise to it.

The challenge for us now is a purposeful one. How might we bring these seven principles into our classrooms and leadership conversations in a way that honours the discipline and offers appropriate challenge for learners? How might we make space for rhetoric to do its quiet, steady work of deepening understanding and strengthening judgement?

There are no quick fixes here, nor do there need to be. What this book offers is a direction of travel, grounded in evidence and trust. If we take it seriously, it will enrich not only our curriculum but the wider lives of the young people we teach.

Bibliography

Arendt, H. (1958) *The human condition*, University of Chicago Press, Chicago.

Aristotle (1926) *Rhetoric*, J. Freese (trans.), Loeb Classical Library, Harvard University Press, Cambridge.

Aristotle (1932) *Politics*, H. Rackham (trans.), Loeb Classical Library, Harvard University Press, Cambridge.

Aristotle (1934) *Nicomachean ethics*, H. Rackham (trans.), Loeb Classical Library, Harvard University Press, Cambridge.

Arnold, M. (1873) *Culture and anarchy*, Cambridge University Press, Cambridge.

Asen, R. (2004) 'A discourse theory of citizenship', *Quarterly Journal of Speech*, 90, 2, 189–211.

Ashley, M. (2005) 'Tensions between indoctrination and the development of judgement: The case against early closure', *Environmental Education Research*, 11, 2, 187–197.

Barnes, C. (2005) 'Critical thinking revisited: Its past, present and future', *New Directions for Community Colleges*, 130, 5–13.

Barnett, S.M. and Ceci, S.J. (2002) 'When and where do we apply what we learn?: A taxonomy for far transfer', *Psychological Bulletin*, 128, 4, 612.

Benhabib, S. (1996) 'Toward a deliberative model of democratic legitimacy', in S. Benhabib (ed.), *Democracy and difference: Contesting the boundaries of the political*, Princeton University Press, Princeton, New Jersey.

Benhabib, S. (2002) *The claims of culture: Equality and diversity in the global era*, Princeton University Press, Princeton, New Jersey.

Benson, T. and Prosser, M. (1972) *Readings in classical rhetoric*, Indiana University Press, Bloomington and London.

Bentley, R. (2004) 'Rhetorical democracy', in B. Fontana, C.J. Nederman and G. Remer (eds.), *Talking democracy: Historical perspectives on rhetoric and democracy*, Pennsylvania State University Press, Pennsylvania, 115–134.

Berlin, J. (1988) 'Rhetoric and ideology in the writing class', *College English*, 50, 5, 477–494.

Berlin, J. (1996) *Rhetorics, poetics and cultures*, National Council of Teachers of English, Urbana, IL.

Bernstein, B. (2000) *Pedagogy, symbolic control, and identity*, Rowman & Littlefield Publishers, Lanham, Maryland.

Beyer, B. (1988) *Developing a thinking skills program*, Allyn and Bacon, Boston.

Bickmore, K. (2008) 'Human rights, identities and conflict management: A study of school culture as experienced through classroom relationships', in J. Arthur and I. Davies (eds.), *Citizenship education*, Vol. 4, Sage Publishers, London.

Biesta, G. (2008) 'What kind of citizen? What kind of democracy? Citizenship education and the Scottish curriculum for excellence', *Scottish Educational Review*, 40, 2, 38–52.

Biesta, G. (2011) *Learning democracy in school and society: Education, lifelong learning, and the politics of citizenship*, Sense Publishers, Rotterdam.

Bizzell, P. and Herzberg, B. (1990) *The rhetorical tradition: Readings from classical times to the present*, st, Martin's Press Inc, Boston.

Bohman, J. (1996) *Public deliberation: pluralism, complexity, and democracy*, MIT Press, Cambridge.

Bohman, J. (1998) 'The coming of age of deliberative democracy', *Journal of Political Philosophy*, 6, 4, 400–425.

Bonazzi M., Dorion, L., Hatano, T., Notomi, N. and Van Ackeren, M. (2009) '"Socratic" dialogues', The Internet Journal of the International Plato Society. Available at: https://www.scribd.com/document/224706955/Collectif-Socratic-Dialogues.

Booth, W. (2004) *The rhetoric of rhetoric; The quest for effective communication*, Wiley-Blackwell, Oxford.

Bourelle, A. (2009) 'Lessons from Quintilian: Writing and rhetoric across the curriculum for the modern university', *Currents in Teaching and Learning*, 1, 2, 28–36.

Britton, J. (1970) *Language and learning*, University of Miami Press, Coral Gables, FL.

Brown, K. (1998) *Education, culture and critical thinking*, Ashgate Publishing, Aldershot.

Brown, K. and Fairbrass, S. (2009) *The citizenship teacher's handbook*, Continuum Publishers, London.

Browne, M. and Keeley, S. (1986) *Asking the right questions: A guide to critical thinking*, 2nd edition, Prentice-Hall Publishers, New Jersey.

Carpini, M., Cook, F. and Jacobs, L. (2004) 'Public deliberations, discursive participation and citizen engagement: a review of the empirical literature', *Annual Review of Political Science*, 7, 315–344.

Chaffee, J. (1992) 'Teaching critical thinking across the curriculum', *New Directions for Community Colleges*, 77, 25–35.

Chambers (1996) *Reasonable democracy: Jürgen Habermas and the politics of discourse*, Cornwell University Press, Ithaca.

Chambers (2009) 'Rhetoric and the public sphere: Has deliberative democracy abandoned mass democracy', *Political Theory*, 37, 3, 323–350. https://doi.org/10.1177/0090591709332336

Chambers, S. (2003) 'Deliberative democratic theory', *Annual Review of Political Science*, 6, 1, 307–326.

Chan, J., Fancourt, N. and Guilfoyle, L. (2021) 'Argumentation in religious education in England: An Analysis of locally agreed syllabuses', *British Journal of Religious Education*, 43, 4, 458–471.

Chater, M. (2020) *Reforming RE: Power and knowledge in a worldviews curriculum*, John Catt, Woodbridge.

Christodoulou, D. (2014) *Seven Myths About Education*, Routledge, London.

Cicero (1939) *Brutus and orator*, G. Hendrickson and H. Hubbell (trans.), Loeb Classical Library, Harvard University Press, Cambridge.

Cicero (1948) *de oratore*, E. Sutton and H. Rackham (trans.), Loeb Classical Library, Harvard University Press, Cambridge.

Cicero (1968) *de Inventione, de optimo genere; oratorium topica*, H. Hubbell (trans.), Loeb Classical Library, Harvard University Press, Cambridge.

Clarke, M. (1996) *Rhetoric at Rome: A historical survey*, Routledge, London.

Connolly, J. (2007) *The state of speech: Rhetorical and political thought in ancient Rome*, Princeton University Press, Princeton, New Jersey.

Cooper, K. and White, R. (2006) *The practical critics educator*, Springer, Dordecht.

Counsell, C., (2018) 'Taking curriculum seriously', *Impact*, 4, 6–9.

Counsell, C., (2020) *The indirect manifestation of knowledge: final performance as deceiver and guide*. Available at: https://thedignityofthethingblog.wordpress.com/

Counsell, C., https://thedignityofthethingblog.wordpress.com/ January 2020.

Covey, S. R. (2012) *The wisdom and teachings of Stephen R. Covey*, Simon and Schuster.

Crick, B. (1998) *Education for citizenship and the teaching of democracy in schools: Final report of the advisory group on citizenship*, Qualifications and Curriculum Authority, London.

Crick, B. (2000) *Essays on citizenship*, Continuum Publishers, London.

Crick, B. (2008) 'Democracy', in J. Arthur, I. Davies and C. Hahn (eds.), *The Sage handbook of education for citizenship and democracy*, Sage Publishers, London, 13–19.

Crowley, S. and Hawhee, D. (2012) *Ancient rhetorics for contemporary students*, Pearson, Upper Saddle River, New Jersey.

Crystal, D. (2002) *The English Language: A guided tour of the Language*, Penguin, UK.

Department for Education (2025, March 18) *Curriculum and assessment review: Interim report*. UK Government. Available at: https://assets.publishing.service.gov.uk/media/6821d69eced319d02c9060e3/Curriculum_and_Assessment_Review_interim_report.pdf

Department for Education (2003) *21st century skills: Realising our potential*. Available at: 21st century skills: realising our potential - GOV.UK.

Department for Education (2025) *The Writing Framework*. Accessed online at https://assets.publishing.service.gov.uk/media/68bec95444fd43581bda1c86/The_writing_framework_092025.pdf (10th October 2025)

Deuchar, R. (2003) 'Preparing tomorrow's people: The new challenges of citizenship education for involving Scottish pupils and teachers in participative decision-making processes', *Scottish Educational Review*, 35, 1, 27–37.

Dewey, J. (1927) *The public and its problems*, Swallow Press, Chicago.

Diodorus (2010) *Biblioteca historica: The Persian wars to the fall of Athens*, University of Texas Press, Austin.

Dryzek, J. (2000) *Deliberative democracy and beyond: Liberals, critics, contestations*, Oxford University Press, Oxford.

Dryzek, J. (2010) 'Rhetoric in democracy: A systemic appreciation', *Political Theory*, 38, 3, 319–339.

Ennis, R. (1962) 'A concept of critical thinking', *Harvard Educational Review*, 32, 1, 81–111.

Ennis, R. (1981) 'Rational thinking and educational practice', in J. Soltis (ed.), *Philosophy and education*, Eightieth yearbook for the National Society for the Study of Education, part 1, National Society for the Study of Education, Chicago, 143–183.

Enslin, P. and White, P. (2003) 'Democratic citizenship', in N. Blake, P. Smeyers, R. Smith and P. Standish (eds.), *The Blackwell guide to the philosophy of education*, Blackwell Publishing, Oxford, 110–125.

Fleming, D. (1988) 'Rhetoric as a course of study', *College English*, 61, 169–191.

Fleming, D. (2003) 'Becoming rhetorical: An education in the topics', in J. Petraglia and D. Bahri (eds.), *The realms of rhetoric*, State University of New York Press, Albany, 93–116.

Fontana, B., Nederman, C.J. and Remer, G. (2004) Talking democracy: historical perspectives on rhetoric and democracy, Pennsylvania State University Press, Pennsylvania.

Francis, B. (2025a, March 18). We'll resist 'non-educationalists' who want revolution. *Tes Magazine*. Retrieved from https://www.tes.com/magazine/analysis/general/becky-francis-changes-in-curriculum-assessment-review

Francis, B. (2025b) *Curriculum and Assessment Review Final Report: Building a world class curriculum for all*, Department for Education, London.

Galston, W. (1989) 'Civic education in the liberal state', in N. Rosenblum (ed.), *Liberalism and the moral life*, Harvard University Press, Cambridge, 89–102.

Gaonkar, D. (1990) 'Rhetoric and its double: Reflections on the rhetorical turn in the human sciences', in H. Simons (ed.), *The rhetorical turn: Invention and persuasion in the conduct of inquiry*, University of Chicago Press, Chicago, 341–366.

Garsten, B. (2009) *Saving persuasion: A defense of rhetoric and judgment*, Harvard University Press, Cambridge.

Gurak, L. (2004) 'Cyberliteracy: Toward a new rhetorical consciousness', in C. Glenn, M. Lyday and W. Sharer (eds.), *Rhetorical education in America*, University of Alabama Press, Tuscaloosa, 179–197.

Habermas, J. (1993) *Justification and application: Remarks on discourse ethics*, C. Cronin (trans.), Polity Press, Cambridge.

Hansen, K. (2012) 'Deliberative democracy: Mapping out the deliberative turn in democratic theory', in C. Kock and L. Villadsen (eds.), *Rhetorical citizenship and public deliberation*, Pennsylvania State University Press, Pennsylvania, 13–27.

Hauser, G. (2008) 'Rethinking deliberative democracy: Rhetoric, power and civil society', in T. McDorman and D. Timmerman (eds.), *Rhetoric and democracy: Pedagogical and political practices*, Michigan State University Press, East Lansing, 225–264.

Hauser, G. and Benoit-Barne, C. (2002) 'Reflections on rhetoric, deliberative democracy, civil society, and trust', *Rhetoric and Public Affairs*, 5, 2, 261–275.

Hazell, W. (2020) 'State school teaches Aristotle to 11-year-olds because they felt patronised by modern texts', *The iPaper*, 12th February. Available at: State school teaches Aristotle to 11-year-olds because they felt patronised by modern texts.

Healy, P. (2011) 'Rethinking deliberative democracy: From deliberative discourse to transformative dialogue', *Philosophy and Social Criticism*, 37, 295–311.

Hicks, D. (2002) 'The promise(s) of deliberative democracy', *Rhetoric and Public Affairs*, 5, 2, 223–260.

Hill, C. and Howard, K. (2020) *Symbiosis: The curriculum and the classroom*, John Catt.

Hirsch, E.D., Kett, J.F. and Trefil, J.S. (1988). *The dictionary of cultural literacy*, Houghton Miffler Harcourt, Boston

Hogan, J. (2008) 'Rhetorical pedagogy and democratic citizenship: Revising the traditions of civic engagement and public deliberation', in T. McDorman and D. Timmerman (eds.), *Rhetoric and democracy: Pedagogical and political practices*, Michigan State University Press, East Lansing, 75–98.

Holmes-Henderson, A. and Tempest, K. (2018) 'Classics and twenty-first-century skills' in A. Holmes-Henderson, S. Hunt and M. Musié (eds.) *Forward with Classics. Classical languages in schools and communities,* 231–242, Bloomsbury academic, London.

Holmes-Henderson, A. (2025) 'Not seeing the wood for DAFOREST: Rhetoric in the English classroom', *English in Education*, 59(4), 298–303. https://doi.org/10.1080/04250494.2025.2563610

Howard, K. (2019) *Stop talking about wellbeing: A pragmatic approach to teacher workload*, John Catt, Melton.

Ivie, R. (2002) 'Rhetorical deliberation and democratic politics in the here and now', *Rhetoric and Public Affairs*, 5, 2, 277–285.

Jones, E. and Jones, N. (1992) *Education for citizenship: Ideas and perspectives for cross-curricular study*, Kogan Page, London.

Jost, W. and Hyde, M. (1997) *Rhetoric and hermeneutics in our time: A reader*, Yale University Press, New Haven and London.

Kahneman, D., Rosenfield, A.M., Gandhi, L. and Blaser, T. (2016) 'Noise: How to overcome the high, hidden cost of inconsistent decision making', *Harvard Business Review*, 94, 10, 38–46.

Kant, I. (1951) *Critique of judgement*, J. Bernard (trans.), Hafner Press, New York.

Kant, I. (2007) *Critique of pure reason*, Translated, Edited and with an Introduction by M. Weigelt, Penguin, London.

Knight, C. (1992) 'Teaching critical thinking in the social sciences', *New Directions for Community Colleges*, 77, 63–73.

Knight, J. and Johnson, J. (1997) 'What sort of equality does deliberative democracy require?', in J. Bohman and W. Rehg (eds.), *Essays on reason and politics: Deliberative democracy*, MIT Press, Cambridge, 279–316.

Kock, C. and Villadsen, L. (2012) *Rhetorical citizenship and public deliberation*, Pennsylvania State University Press, Pennsylvania.

Kueh, R. and Chater, M. (2020) *A Disciplinary Hearing' in Chater, M. (ed.) Reforming RE: Reforming religious education: Power and knowledge in a worldviews curriculum*, John Catt, Melton.

Kugelmass, J. (2008) 'Stop using rhetoric to teach writing', *Inside Higher Ed blog*. http://www.insidehighered.com/views/2008/12/23/kugelmass.

Kymlicka, W. and Norman, W. (1994) 'Return of the citizen: A survey of recent work on citizenship theory', *Ethics*, 104, 352–381.

Lancaster, S. (2022) *Connect: How to Inspire, Influence and Energise Anyone, Anywhere, Anytime*, Heligo Books, London.

Leith, S. (2011) *You talkin' to me? Rhetoric from Aristotle to Obama*, Profile Books, London.

Livingstone (1941) *President of Corpus Christi College*, address in Oxford.

Manin, B. (1987) 'On legitimacy and political deliberation', *Political Theory*, 15, 3, 338–368.

McDorman, T. and Timmerman, D. (2008) *Rhetoric and democracy: pedagogical and political practices*, Michigan State University Press, East Lansing.

Marzano, R., Pickering, D. and McTighe, J. (1993) *Assessing student outcomes: Performance assessment using the dimensions of learning model*, Association for supervision and curriculum development, Alexandria.

McCarthy, T. (1975) *Legitimation crisis*, Beacon Press, Boston.

McDonald, J. (2012) 'I agree, but ... finding alternatives to controversial projects through public deliberation', in C. Kock and L. Villadsen (eds.), *Rhetorical citizenship and public deliberation*, Pennsylvania State University Press, Pennsylvania, 199–217.

McKerrow, R. (1998) 'Rhetoric and the construction of a deliberative community', *Southern Communication Journal*, 63, 4, 350–356.

McLaughlin, T. (1992) 'Citizenship, diversity and education: A philosophical perspective', *Journal of Moral Education*, 21, 3, 235–250.

Muller, J. (2014) Every picture tells a story: Epistemological access and knowledge, *Education as Change*, 18, 2, 255–269, https://doi.org/10.1080/16823206.2014.932256

Murphy, J. (2012) *A short history of writing instruction from Ancient Greece to contemporary America*, Routledge, New York.

Neel, J. (1988) *Plato, Derrida, and writing*, Southern Illinois University Press, Carbondale.

Newlands, C. and Murphy, J. (2010) *Arguments in rhetoric against Quintilian. Translation and text of Peter Ramus' Rhetoricae Distinctiones in Quintilianum*, Southern Illinois University Press, Carbondale.

Norval, A. (2007) *Aversive democracy*, Cambridge University Press, Cambridge.

Nussbaum, M. (1986) *The fragility of goodness: Luck and ethics in Greek tragedy and philosophy*, Cambridge University Press, Cambridge.

Nussbaum, M. (1997) *Cultivating humanity: a classical defence of reform in liberal education*, Harvard University Press, Cambridge.

Nussbaum, M. (2010) *Not for profit: Why democracy needs the humanities*, Princeton University Press, New Jersey.

Ober, J. (2005) *Athenian legacies: Essays on the politics of going on together*, Princeton University Press, New Jersey.

Ofsted. (2021). *Research Review Series: Religious Education* Available at: (Accessed: 08/03/2024) https://www.gov.uk/government/publications/research-review-series-religious-education

Ofsted. (2024, March 5). *Telling the story: The English education subject report.* Research and analysis. Retrieved from https://www.gov.uk/government/publications/subject-report-series-english/telling-the-story-the-english-education-subject-report

Oracy Education Commission. (2024, October). *We need to talk: The report of the Commission on the Future of Oracy Education in England.* Retrieved from https://oracyeducation commission.co.uk/wp-content/uploads/2024/10/Future-of-Oracy-v23-web-13.pdf

Ovid (1916) *Metamorphoses Books IX-XV*, G. Goold and F. Miller (trans.), Loeb Classical Library, Harvard University Press, Cambridge.

Paul, R. (2005) 'The state of critical thinking today', *New Directions for Community Colleges*, 130, 27–38.

Pernot, L. (2005) *Rhetoric in antiquity*, Catholic University of America Press, Washington, D.C.

Plato (1925) *Lysis, Symposium and Gorgias*, W. Lamb (trans.), Loeb Classical Library, Harvard University Press, Cambridge.

Plato (1929) *Timaeus, Critias, Cleitophon, Menexenus and Epistles*, R. Bury (trans.), Loeb Classical Library, Harvard University Press, Cambridge.

Plato (1983) *Hippias Major*, Hackett Publishing, Cambridge, MA.

Plato (1989) *Theaetetus*, H. Fowler (trans.), Loeb Classical Library, Harvard University Press, Cambridge.

Plato (1999) *Euthyphro, Apology, Crito, Phaedo and Phaedrus*, H. Fowler (trans.), Loeb Classical Library, Harvard University Press, Cambridge.

Poulakos, T. (1987) 'Isocrates's use of narrative in the "Evagoras": Epideictic rhetoric and moral action', *Quarterly Journal of Speech*, 73, 317–328.

Powell, E. (1968) 'Rivers of Blood' speech, delivered to a Conservative Association meeting in Birmingham on April 20th 1968. Available at: https://anth1001.wordpress.com/wp-content/uploads/2014/04/enoch-powell_speech.pdf

Putnam, R. (2000) *Bowling alone: The collapse and revival of American community*, Simon and Schuster, New York.

Putnam, R. and Feldstein, L. (2003) *Better together: Restoring the American community*, Simon and Schuster, New York.

Quintilian (1980) *Instituto oratoria*, H. Butler (trans.), Loeb Classical Library, Harvard University Press, Cambridge.

Remer, G. (1999) 'Political oratory and conversation: Cicero versus deliberative democracy', *Political Theory*, 27, 1, 39–64.

Remer, G. (2000) 'Two models of deliberation and the ratification of the constitution', *Journal of Political Philosophy*, 8, 1, 68–90.

Robinson, M. (2013) *Trivium*, Independent Thinking Press, Carmarthen.

Ross, A. (2008) *A European education: Citizenship, identities and young people*, Trentham Books, Stoke-on-Trent.

Ross, H. and Munn, P. (2008) 'Representing self-in-society: education for citizenship and the social subjects curriculum in Scotland', *Journal of Curriculum Studies*, 40, 2, 251–275.

Schiappa, E. (1999) *The beginnings of rhetorical theory in classical Greece*, Yale University Press, New Haven and London.

Scott, W. (1854) *Daniel, a model for young men*, Log College Press, Pennsylvania.

Sharples, J., Albers, B. and Fraser, S. (2018) *Putting evidence to work: A school's guide to implementation*. Guidance Report. Education Endowment Foundation.

Sharples, J., Eaton, J. and Boughelaf, J. (2024) *A school's guide to implementation. Guidance report, Education Endowment Foundation.*

Shiffman, G. (2004) 'Deliberation versus decision: Platonism in contemporary democratic theory', in B. Fontana, C. Nederman and G. Remer (eds.), *Talking democracy:*

Historical perspectives on rhetoric and democracy, Pennsylvania State University Press, Pennsylvania, 87–114.

Shor, I. and Pari, C. (1999) *Critical literacy in action*, Heinemann, Portsmouth, New Hampshire.

Simpson, L. (2001) *The unfinished project: Toward a postmetaphysical humanism*, Routledge, London.

Steel, C. (2001) *Cicero, rhetoric, and empire*, Oxford University Press, Oxford.

Stevens, L. and Bean, T. (2007) *Critical literacy: Context, research and practice in the k-12 classroom*, Sage Publications, London.

Stroh, W. (1975) *Taxis Und Taktik: Die Advokat. Dispositionskunst in Ciceros Gerichtsreden*, Teubner, Stuttgart.

Suto, I. (2013) Twenty first-century skills: ancient, ubiquitous, enigmatic? *Cambridge Assessment*. Available at: https://doi.org/10.17863/CAM.100282.

Szuplat, T. (2024) Say it well, Ebury Edge, London.

Tacitus (1989) *Agricola, Germania, Dialogus*, M. Hutton and W. Peterson (trans.), Loeb Classical Library, Harvard University Press, Cambridge.

Tell, H. (2009) 'Wisdom for sale? The Sophists and money', *Classical Philology*, 104, 1, 13–33.

Toulmin, S. E. (2003) *The uses of argument*, Cambridge University Press.

Turner, K. (1998) 'Rhetorical studies in the twenty-first century: Envisioning the possibilities', *Southern Communication Journal*, 63, 4, 330–336.

Walton, D. (2004) 'Criteria of rationality for evaluating democratic public rhetoric', in B. Fontana, C. Nederman and G. Remer (eds.), *Talking democracy: Historical perspectives on rhetoric and democracy*, Pennsylvania State University Press, Pennsylvania, 295–330.

Walzer, M. (1989) 'A critique of philosophical conversation', *Philosophical forum*, 21, 1, 182–196.

Wardy, R. (1996) *The birth of rhetoric*, Routledge, London.

Weaver, R., Johannesen, R., Strickland, R. and Eubanks, R. (1970) *Language is sermonic: Richard M. Weaver on the nature of rhetoric*, Louisiana State University Press, Baton Rouge.

Webster, L. (2023) *EMC Approaches to Rhetoric: A Practical Guide for 11-14 year-olds*, English and Media Centre, London.

Welch, K. (1999) *Electric rhetoric: Classical rhetoric, oralism and a new literacy*, The MIT Press, Cambridge, Massachusetts.

Westheimer, J. and Kahne, J. (2004) 'What kind of citizen? The politics of educating for democracy', *American Educational Research Journal*, 41, 2, 237–269.

Wiliam, D. (2013) *Principled curriculum design*, SSAT.

Willingham, D.T. (2008) 'Critical thinking: Why is it so Hard to teach?', *Arts Education Policy Review*, 109, 4, 21–32. http://dx.doi.org/10.3200/AEPR.109.4.21-32

Willingham, D.T. (2019) 'How to teach critical thinking', *Education: Future Frontiers*, 1, 1, 1–17.

Winch, C. (2013) 'Curriculum design and epistemic ascent', *Journal of Philosophy of Education*, 47, 1, 128–146. https://doi.org/10.1111/1467-9752.12006

Yack, B. (2006) 'Rhetoric and public reasoning: An Aristotelian understanding of political deliberation', *Political Theory*, 34, 4, 417–438.

Young, A.M., Battaglia, A. and Cloud, D. (2010) '(Un) Disciplining the scholar activist: policing the boundaries of political engagement', *Quarterly Journal of Speech*, 96, 4, 427–435.

Young, I.M. (1996) 'Communication and the other: Beyond deliberative democracy', in S. Benhabib (ed.), *Democracy and difference: Contesting the boundaries of the political*, Princeton University press, Princeton, New Jersey.

Young, I.M. (1997) *Intersecting voices: Dilemmas of gender, political philosophy and policy*, Princeton University Press, Princeton, New Jersey.

Young, I.M. (2002) *Inclusion and democracy*, Oxford University Press, Oxford.

Zuckerberg, D. (2018) *Not All Dead White Men: Classics and misogyny in the digital age*, Harvard University Press, Cambridge.

Index

www.ingramcontent.com/pod-product-compliance
Lightning Source LLC
LaVergne TN
LVHW060627290826
846781LV00026B/251
9781032529035